WO

Please return/renew this item by the last date shown

worcestershire
countycouncil
Libraries & Learning

700036721038

SHIP MODELS
from Kits

SHIP MODELS
from Kits
BASIC AND ADVANCED
TECHNIQUES FOR
SMALL SCALES

DAVID GRIFFITH

Seaforth
PUBLISHING

Copyright © David Griffith 2009
English translation © Seaforth Publishing 2009

First published in Great Britain in 2009 by
Seaforth Publishing
An imprint of Pen & Sword Books Ltd
47 Church Street, Barnsley
S Yorkshire S70 2AS

www.seaforthpublishing.com
Email info@seaforthpublishing.com

British Library Cataloguing in Publication Data
A CIP data record for this book is available from the British Library

ISBN 978-1-84832-024-6

Typeset and designed by Neil Sayer
Printed and bound in China

Contents

∽ *Introduction* ∽

I have been making models since I was about seven years old, so as I sit writing this, that is about four and a half decades. One of my earliest memories is of standing next to my father, who is sitting at the dining table, gluing together pieces of plastic. Next morning, I get up out of bed and discover a little white Skyhawk waiting for me. On other occasions it is a Spitfire or a Sopwith Camel. My memory fails me when I try to recall how long the undercarriage stayed on that one!

I was hooked straight away, and like any addict, my habit has grown more demanding with the passing of the years. I went through various phases – aircraft and tanks as a child, Historex figures as an adolescent and at university, a couple of wooden farm carts in my mid to late twenties, a rediscovery of plastic after I got married and, in the mid 1990s, an eighteenth-century frigate, plank on frame and fully rigged, that took more than two years to complete.

Since about 2000, I have concentrated on ships and have honed my skills in this less popular genre. I enter and regularly win competitions, and display my models at shows throughout Scotland and northern England, including the International Plastic Modellers' Society (IPMS) Nationals at Telford. In 2008, I even went to America with them!

I thoroughly enjoy talking to people about what I do. Being in no way a professional modeller, I am happy to share my techniques with others. I just want to promote the hobby and allow as many people as possible to get as much enjoyment from it as I do. It is all about having fun, and if that goes, then there is no point in carrying on doing it.

Being asked to write this book came as a complete, but delightful, surprise to me. I was at Scale Modelworld at Telford in November 2007, and was displaying my collection of models. I had copies of a set of notes on my techniques that I was giving away to anyone who was interested. I was approached by Robert Gardiner of Seaforth Publishing, who asked me if I would consider writing something for him. I had to confess that the idea had never crossed my mind. Of course, I do have the next great Booker Prize-winning novel in my head (everyone does have a novel in their head, and in the vast majority of cases, my own included, that is exactly where it should stay), but I had never done any serious writing. That did not put him off; my notes convinced him that I could string enough words together to make a meaningful sentence.

At first it seemed that I might be invited to contribute to one of a series of books that he was publishing, but the idea broadened and blossomed and this humble volume is the result. I use the word humble advisedly, because I know full well that although I am a good modeller, I am not the best in the world, or even this country. I simply happened to be in the right place at the right time. I also have a wife who tells me that it is an honour to be asked, and I have to agree.

It is my personal preference to build models in the weathered and waterline style. The aim is to represent an instant of actual life, frozen in time, with an intense sensation of reality about the model. It is mounted on a realistic sea base. The paintwork uses a variety of techniques to shade and highlight details and to imitate the effects of the weather, sunlight and hard use. Crew figures show human activity. It is this style of modelling that I demonstrate in this book.

This is not to suggest that I do not appreciate the museum style of modelling. I greatly enjoy looking at full hull models, mounted on pedestals or plinths and with pristine paintwork showing off every aspect of the builder's skill. As I write these words, I have just returned from the annual convention of IPMS in the United States, where the 'Best in Show' trophy went to a scratch-built 1/96 scale model of a US destroyer, done in the museum style, and a well-deserved award it was, too.

My intention in this book is to demonstrate some of the techniques of small-scale ship modelling; not only basic construction but also the more advanced methods that I have picked up over the past few years or devised myself. It will be centred on the construction of two ships – one plastic and the other resin – chosen partly because they are fairly typical products of roughly comparable vessels, but mainly because they were sitting in my stash of unmade kits!

I want this book to be a practical guide that any reasonable modeller can get a lot from. I have seen books showing techniques so complex that few people could dream of emulating them. Although my methods are painstaking and often extremely pernickerty, I think that given care, practice and patience, they are within the capabilities of any good modeller. Do not get disheartened if you find that you cannot master all of them straightaway. Keep at it, analyse where you have done well and where you have done less well, and build up your skills incrementally with each kit that you build. It has taken me several years to work out my techniques, and looking at the models I built when I started out in this genre, I can see just how much I have improved. I hope I can get you to progress down this road, or sea lane, faster that I did.

I assume that you, the reader, are not a complete newcomer to the hobby. I suspect that you would not be looking at this book if you had never made a model in your life. I assume that you have built at least a few models, have accumulated a basic toolkit and do not need to be told what a needle file is or how to apply polystyrene cement. This will enable both of us to get into the meatier bits straightaway.

I do not use any complicated equipment. Admittedly I have both an airbrush and a Dremel-type tool. I regard them both as very useful but they are not unusual items on a modeller's bench nowadays. Everything else is readily obtainable in shops or by mail order, and some of it is available for free.

When you have finished reading this book, I hope you will feel inspired to try them out for yourself. If you build on my ideas to develop your own way of solving problems, then I will be only too glad to have helped. If you meet me at one of the model shows in the UK or abroad, show me what you have done. I would be simply delighted to look at it and chat for a while.

Finally, I acknowledge the support and encouragement of my wife, Ellen, during the writing of this book, although she has banned me from starting any new models until I have finished it, and also to thank Jim Baumann, Mike McCabe and Peter Fulgoney for allowing me to use photographs of some of their models.

David Griffith, 2008

A Note on the Photographs

Except where I have credited otherwise, all of the photographs in the book were taken by me on a Canon EOS digital SLR camera, many with a close-up lens. Lighting conditions varied; in all the constructional photographs, a lot of daylight balanced tungsten lighting was used, but in those of *Sydney* daylight played a part as well, because the model was built during the summer. This has resulted in variations in the colour balance in some of the images, particularly those of *Sydney*. I tried to compensate by taking photographs with different colour settings and choosing the one that best matched the object being photographed. I have not always been successful, and if some of the pictures appear to have a yellow or green cast to them, I beg your forgiveness.

Close-up photography, under intense artificial light, is a harsh and unsympathetic critic. It can show up and emphasise every tiny flaw in construction or finish. On many occasions during the construction of these models, I have not noticed paint smudges, glue spots or adherent specks of dust or hairs until the photos pointed them out to me in all their horrific glory! Of course, it was then too late. These imperfections were almost invisible to the naked eye, which has a way of paying attention selectively to those features that are of interest and ignoring the rest. The camera records with dispassionate objectivity and does not allow one to gloss over things.

Two lessons can be learned from this. First, the best instrument for appreciating a model is the human eye. It is only the most exceptional models, and I do not count my own among them, that can truly stand up to judgement through close-up photography.

Second, taking photographs at frequent intervals during the construction of a model may be a good way of assessing the quality of your work, just as long as you are sufficiently disciplined to go back and sort out imperfections before you move on to the next stage. If not, I imagine it could be a most depressing exercise. It might even persuade you to give up modelling entirely and take up something rather easier, such as golf, or fly-fishing!

CHAPTER 1
❧ *What's on the Market?* ❧

I start this book by stating that I believe that now is a very good time to be a ship modeller. Only ten years ago it seemed that the mainstream plastic kit manufacturers had completely stopped producing new ships and were leaving us with the same old mouldings from the 1970s, the 1960s and even earlier. New kits of aircraft, tanks and cars were coming out with the benefit of crisp and highly detailed new moulds, but we were being left behind. For new and interesting ships we had to explore the emerging resin industry, or scratch build, or both.

How things have changed in the intervening few years. The first spark that I noticed was Tamiya re-tooling its 1/700 *Yamato*, and then bringing out excellent kits of *Prinz Eugen* and *Indianapolis*. Dragon has increased its range of modern and WW2 ships. A major new player has emerged in China, in the form of Trumpeter, and certainly seems to currently be leading the pack, although its products do have problems. The Japanese firms are now re-tooling a number of kits of Japanese ships that were originally released in the 1970s, and in particular Aoshima is replacing its poor kits with highly detailed and state of the art ones. Hasegawa is moving into the 1/350 market, and at the time of writing a 1/700 *Repulse* has been released by Tamiya. Many new kits in 1/700 and 1/350 scales are eagerly awaited.

Eastern Europe is also playing its part in this renaissance. Although there are companies producing kits that are crude in the extreme, a couple of producers are issuing kits that are interesting and sometimes first rate.

Although it is outside the scope of this book, I will mention the larger scale vessels that have been released by Revell of Germany in the form of submarines and an S-Boote, and the Elco PT Boat from Italeri.

The resin industry has developed greatly. Because the resin companies are generally a lot smaller than the plastic producers, sometimes one-man-bands, there is a tendency for brands to come and go. But the leading firms are now releasing products that are not only prolific in number and wide in scope, but also far, far more detailed than anything that could be achieved by the traditional injection moulding techniques.

I am not trying to suggest that resin will take over from plastic. I do not think it will, because they are distinct types of product aimed at different parts of the market, albeit with a fair degree of overlap. On the contrary, I would suggest that the current resurgence of ship kit production by the plastic manufacturers is fuelled by the success of the resin market. I do not think that it was necessarily the original cause of it, but both sides of the industry are now gaining benefit from the momentum.

The 'classic' kits that I built as a schoolboy are still available, but are now looking sad and forlorn alongside the new stuff that is appearing.

Let us look at the various manufacturers and try to decide what is good and what is not so good. I should emphasise that what follows are my personal opinions of manufacturers and products. There will be some about which I have no knowledge and cannot offer useful advice.

Plastic kits

Airfix

This once successful company has declined over the years, and has produced few new kits of any kind recently. It has failed to invest in products to anything like the extent of the Japanese companies that stole a march on it in the 1970s. Its ship kits are all from old moulds, some dating back to the early 1960s. Although the company has always had a reputation for accuracy in terms of dimension and outline, most of its kits are now crude and lack detail. A few, such as *Repulse*, *King George V* and *Belfast* are rather newer and can be spruced up to give something very acceptable. But if you want to build an angled-deck *Victorious* or 'County'-class guided-missile destroyer, then an old Airfix kit is the only show in town, and you will need to do a considerable amount of work and use lots of after market parts to bring it up to scratch. From my point of view, life is too short, and I would rather stick to more modern products.

Revell

Most of Revell's ships are from old moulds, of similar vintage to Airfix. Some are in peculiar scales, showing that they were produced in the days when the kit was designed to go into a standard sized box that would fit conveniently on the shelves of the shop. The German branch of Revell has recently produced a first rate 1/350 *Bismarck*, which is much better than the old Tamiya offering, and also 1/72 submarines and an S-Boote, but these are outside the remit of this book.

Tamiya

In the 1970s, Tamiya appeared to enter into an agreement with other Japanese manufacturers – Hasegawa, Fujimi and Aoshima – to each take a share of the Second World War Japanese fleet to produce in a common scale of 1/700. Some British, US and German ships were included in the range. Of the four companies, Tamiya undoubtedly

1.

Here are a few parts of Tamiya's USS *Missouri*. The decks have fine engraving with grooves between the planks so that a wash will behave predictably. Splinter shields are properly vertical and not significantly thicker towards the base. They are about as thin as can reasonably be achieved with injection moulding. There is room for improvement, because lockers, hatches and watertight doors lack detail. On other parts in the kit the superstructure sides look a bit bland and there are still some of the dreaded 'Aztec stairs' to be dealt with. In general, though, this is an excellently produced kit and much better than those dating from the 1970s.

produced the best kits, followed by Hasegawa and Fujimi, with Aoshima in last place. They show features that might now be thought unfortunate, such as vertical superstructure sides that are bare of detail and slope slightly inwards to enable them to be removed from the moulds, and heavy deck patterns. However, with appropriate photo-etch, and replacement of smaller parts with resin bits, they can be made into very attractive models, and some excellent examples can be found on the web. The 1/700 *Yamato* was re-tooled several years ago, and the *Mogami*-class cruisers have recently had the same treatment with striking results. Completely new 1/700 kits have appeared recently. It appears that Tamiya has been persuaded to get back into ships again, and this must be welcomed.

Tamiya's 1/350 ships are now looking rather tired, but I suspect it will be a long time before they are re-tooled.

Hasegawa

Hasegawa's 1/700 kits were inferior to Tamiya's, but it has recently re-tooled *Ise* and *Hyuga* to a standard that is equal to its rival's newer productions, and have just released *Akagi* in a prewar configuration. It has also taken a leap into 1/350 scale, presumably following the lead of Trumpeter. An interesting subject is the pre-dreadnought *Mikasa*, which was thought by some to be the best ship kit ever produced. It has been followed by others and each has had dedicated photo-etched frets produced that are available separately.

Aoshima

This company's original 1/700 kits from the 1970s were poorly detailed and toy-like. However, it has recently re-tooled *Fuso*, *Yamashiro* and some cruisers, and these are now first-rate modern kits. We must hope the trend continues.

Pit Road/Skywave

I have always understood that this Japanese firm produces kits under the name Pit Road for the home market and Skywave for export. It has a massive range of 1/700 kits, concentrating on Japanese and US subjects. Its kits have a distinctive 'look' about them. You can always tell a Skywave ship! They have some rather annoying idiosyncrasies: irritating raised rims around location holes, scuttles (portholes) that are twice as big as they should be, and they are particular offenders with regard to the sloping verticals, having very oddly shaped gun tubs and splinter shields. Despite this, they are well worth looking at. Pit Road mouldings have also turned up under other makers labels. Tamiya's USS *Bogue* is one, and I am sure that some of Dragon's premium kits are originally Pit Road, albeit with some photo-etched goodies.

Dragon

This Chinese manufacturer had a reputation for poor fit of parts, but in recent years seems to have been in the lead in the introduction of new slide moulding technology. As a result, one is able to mould detail in positions and on faces of parts that would have been totally impossible with two-part moulds. The company seems to try to get the maximum use out of its moulds. Exactly the same sprue will appear in several different kits. The result

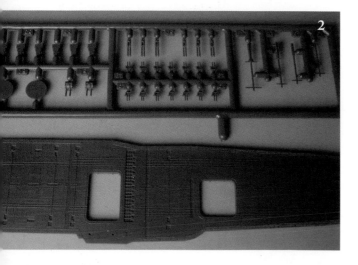

2.

2.

Hasegawa's aircraft carrier *Kaga* is one of its kits from the 1970s and is illustrated for comparison with more up-to-date kits. Detailing is heavy and includes raised lines for the deck markings. The anti-aircraft guns appear clumsy when set against modern offerings, although even those would not match the delicacy of photo-etched items. I suspect that kits such as this will be replaced by new toolings over the next few years.

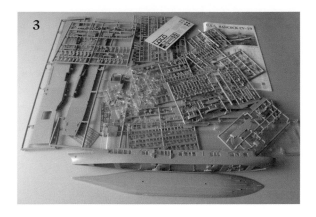

3.

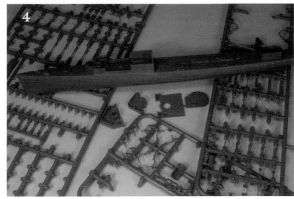

4.

How many parts in this kit? Answers on a postcard, please! If you can't quite make it out in the photo, there are eighteen sprues of plastic and two of brass. That is a total of over 640 parts, including a rather gimmicky transparent flight deck. Dragon's USS *Hancock* is a feast for modellers who enjoy a really full box! It is a kit that will repay having time and care taken over it.

This is work in progress. I am converting Mirage's HMS *Montgomery* to HMS *Lincoln*. I made this choice because an old gentleman of my acquaintance told me he served on this ship as a signaller. It will therefore be emblazoned with his initials in signal flags! I also lived in Lincoln for a few years, so that is another good reason for my choice.

has been a series of variants of the *Essex*-class carriers. Sometimes a whole sprue will be included in the box for the sake of just a couple of parts. This may seem wasteful, although good for the spares box, but is not if the alternative would be to cut a whole new mould. I have yet to build one of these kits, but it is on my 'to do' list. The recently released USS *Buchanan* is regarded as stunning, as is the new *Akagi*.

Trumpeter

This Chinese manufacturer has emerged as a major player in the past few years and brings out new kits at a bewildering rate in both 1/700 and 1/350 scales. The kits are variable in quality, with some having significant problems with fit of parts, engineering and poor levels of detail. But Trumpeter has been tackling subjects that have been ignored by other firms, and so far it has resisted the temptation to give us another *Yamato* or *Bismarck*. I would strongly suggest the reading of reviews of particular kits from this company before making your choice.

Eastern Europe

Old moulds from defunct producers such as Frog have been acquired by various firms in Russia and Eastern Europe and used to re-release some of the old classics. But, unless you are looking for something cheap and cheerful, and are not bothered about detail, you are going to be facing something of an 'adventure'. A few firms are producing their own moulds but quality is not as high as in current kits from the Far East, although some subjects are interesting, such as Tsarist pre-dreadnoughts.

A couple of manufacturers are worthy of special mention. ICM, from Ukraine, produced very impressive kits of German First World War battleships. It may have gone out of business, but its kits are often available, particularly at model shows. Mirage, from Poland, has released some interesting models of flush-decked US destroyers. The breakdown of parts is a bit crude by current standards, but they are fairly crisply moulded and certainly worth consideration. These kits are also being sold under the Airfix label, and I have been led to believe that Mirage's moulds have been sold on to them.

❦ *Resin kits* ❦

The industry that produces resin kits and accessories is profuse and diverse, not only in terms of subject matter, but also with regard to geography and quality. In the past, it has been unfavourably compared to the plastic industry, but this is unfair to both because they are so different.

Plastic manufacturers rely on high sales to give a return on the investment in expensive moulds and machinery. They have to choose popular subjects and that is why we see so many versions of *Yamato*. The same kit is often remoulded and reissued many times over the course of decades.

Resin kit production is a true 'cottage industry'. The companies typically consist of just a few people, who hand build master models and use rubber moulds to produce the resin parts. The flexible rubber moulds enable exquisite levels of detail to be achieved, and shapes that would be impossible to make with injection moulding. Although professional casters may be employed, the process is small scale and labour intensive. The moulds do not last long and production runs are very short, sometimes numbering only a few dozen. Because the initial outlay is minuscule when compared to the cost of making a metal mould for injection moulding, resin producers can afford to take risks with unusual subjects, and respond quickly to modellers' clamourings for a particular ship.

Quality of resin ship kits is dependent upon the skill of the person making the master model and the other processes springing from this, and because people get better with practice, it will be found that the early products of a manufacturer will not be as good as more recent products. It is worthwhile bearing this in mind when looking at product lists; the later kits will almost always be more satisfactory. This is the case even with the most prestigious of the resin manufacturers.

Resin kits are almost always more expensive than a plastic kit of similar size, sometimes three times as much, although detail is usually much finer (bearing in mind the previous paragraph). But I do not think that the producers are exploiting the purchaser. I do not imagine that the resin ship industry has allowed anyone to make a fortune, and for many it is a hobby or a pleasant sideline going along with their main job. I, for one, do not begrudge the money that I give to the resin boys, whether it is at a model show or over the Internet. They are the oxygen of our hobby.

Let us look at individual manufacturers. I also mention those that produce after-market parts.

White Ensign

The largest player in the UK concentrates largely on British subjects, with a scattering of US and German subjects. They (and I use the plural deliberately, knowing the people involved) produce their own kits along with photo-etch sets, resin accessories and paints, and also stock a vast range of other firms' products, which they distribute worldwide by a very efficient mail order service. I find that their resin kits have detail that is a little less crisp than some other makers, but their photo-etch is as good as any in the world. Their more recent kits are very complete, and you know that

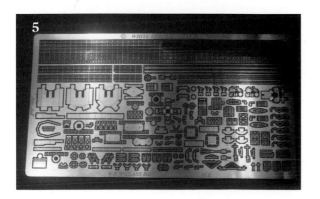

5.

This is White Ensign's new fret for the Tamiya 1/700-scale V&W-class destroyers. The brass sheet is considerably bigger than the kit on which it is intended to go. It contains enough parts to do at least two complete models and has parts for all the various conversions carried out on these ships during the Second World War. In my opinion, this represents outstanding value for money.

6.

Photography cannot do justice to the quality of casting on the latest Combrig kits, such as HMS *Indomitable*. These are only a sample of the parts. The decks feature engraved covers for the coal chutes that are only visible with good light. Its kits are usually very well engineered and fit perfectly. Although I have yet to build this kit, I expect it will be no different.

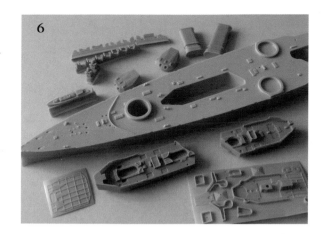

you will have to add very little to a White Ensign kit. All of the kits contain railings – something that other producers expect you to provide yourself. White Ensign tends to bring out excellent dedicated photo-etched sets for many new kits soon after they are released. The availability of such add-ons is an important consideration when choosing what kit to buy. Some of their photo-etch is deliciously fiddly, requiring multiple folds of a single part. Great fun!

L'Arsenal

This French firm not only produces some of the finest resin accessories available but also makes kits. It has predominantly French and British subjects, with some crossover, and chooses subjects not tackled by other producers. Its HMS *Colossus* is particularly attractive.

Combrig

This Russian firm is among my favourites. Although its early kits need a lot of work, more recent releases feature some of the finest resin

casting in the hobby, and some of the best value for money. I particularly recommend Combrig's US destroyers for beginners to resin, but one should get some experience before tackling its recent battleships or cruisers, which are exquisite but with huge numbers of parts.

Samek

This Czech producer has gone out of business, but its kits can sometimes be found, and feature particularly crisp moulding with very sharp corners. HMS *Royal Oak* is well worth snapping up if you run across it.

NNT Modell

Norbert Thiel produces a style of kit that is very similar to Samek, and I wonder if they have been connected in some way. His kits are crisp and straightforward, forming the basis for a very good model. The resin kit that I build later in this book is an NNT product.

7.

I think that USS *Hughes* is the best of Niko's destroyer kits that I have examined. The amount of detail cast onto the one-piece hull and superstructure, and including all the undercuts, would be impossible to achieve in an injection-moulded kit. It gives hull scuttles in a straight line in this kit. The smallest parts are so delicate that you can hardly believe them. I'm rather looking forward to this little one, not least because of a fancy colour scheme.

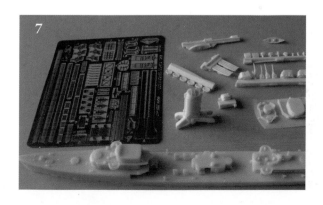

Niko

This is a Polish company that manages to mould an extraordinary amount of detail onto a single part. The result is impressive but fragile. These sometimes have problems with platforms that are slightly bent or hull scuttles that are out of line and in need of filling and re-drilling. With a little effort very good results can be obtained. Niko has also begun producing resin replacement parts, such as AA guns with astounding detail, and I cannot recommend these highly enough.

HP Models

HP has a vast range of kits of unusual subjects in its list. Its more recent releases have sharp moulding, but, generally, they have less detail than many other producers and require more input from the modeller. They usually contain no photo-etch. I would suggest modellers acquire some resin experience before tackling one of these kits.

Admiralty Model Works

This is a fairly new firm from the United States. It has only released a few kits, but its sights are firmly fixed at the top end of the market. Its kits are carefully researched, moulded with enormous detail all round and very complete, requiring only glue, paint and rigging materials from the modeller. I suggest watching very closely.

Loose Cannon

This is a fascinating US company that concentrates on accessories for dioramas such as dockside buildings, cranes, etc., as well as less mainstream ships, especially merchantmen. Its kits will need more work from the modeller, but I have seen some most attractive results.

8.

Pavel from Admiralty Model Works has reduced the amount of work needed in construction of HMS *Glorious* by including so much in the single piece casting of the hull and superstructure. But he makes the painting 'challenging'. The steam pipes, moulded integrally onto the funnel, are cast with hollow ends, and the same goes for the 4in gun barrels, although the naked eye can hardly see it.

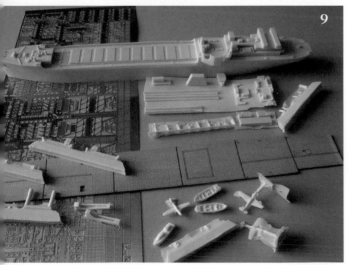

9.

The standard of resin casting on Loose Cannon kits is not as good as many other firms, but this is offset by an interesting choice of subjects. This is *Langley*, the US Navy's first aircraft carrier. The resin parts will need some work to refine the detail, but the kit also includes an enormous photo-etched fret and a laser-cut wooden deck. It can be built into a most attractive model, and such an example won a silver medal at the US National Convention in 2008.

❧ *After-market parts* ❧

I mention above some of the firms that produce accessories alongside their kits. There are also producers that make only accessories, both resin and photo-etch.

Gold Medal Models

Loren Perry has been established for many years as one of the world's best photo-etch makers. He produces parts that are mainly aimed at improving US and Japanese ships, although there are very useful parts for British ships too. He chiefly uses stainless steel. As a result, part are harder to cut, but are much more robust than brass. His 'ultra-fine' railings are more delicate than any other. Some of the older sets, which had been looking a bit crude, are being updated to the highest standard.

Lion Roar

This Chinese manufacturer now produces photo-etch sets profusely. Alongside generic shapes, useful for scratch-builders, and replacements for particular items such as AA guns and radars, it produces details for some of the newer 1/350-scale kits. These are enormously complex, with multiple sets for each ship. To use them all would cost more than the price of the basic kit and stretch the skills of any but the best modeller. The few sets that I have used from Lion Roar have been made of very soft brass that distorts a bit too easily. But I particularly like the 1/700 crew figures. These avoid the stereotyped poses of other producers.

Voyager

This is another Chinese company that produces accessories in both resin and photo-etch. Most of its products are replacement items rather than dedicated frets for particular kits. The range is mainly for Japanese and US ships. The items that I

10.

This is Gold Medal's set for Second World War British warships. It contains cranes, catapults, ladders, funnel cages and plenty of railings that have the correct stanchion spacing. I always have a set or two of these in my photo-etch stash.

have seen lead me to think that they are a bit more complex and detailed than Lion Roar and are on slightly more robust brass.

Eduard

This Czech company has been around for a long time. It makes brass parts for armour and aircraft kits, but has some for ships as well. Several products are now supplied ready painted, and although most seatbelts and instrument panels are not going to be of use for ship modelling, pre-painted crew figures certainly are. Nevertheless, I find the colours a touch bright and in need of a wash of oil paint for these to be toned down.

11.

Eduard's fret of crew figures gives enough men to populate quite a few ships. I still think there are too many waving their arms in the air, but at least there are only eight that are saluting!

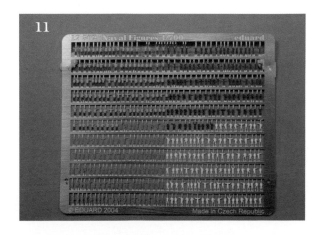

There is a large number of other manufacturers around, based in the United States, Europe and, to a lesser extent, the Far East. I have not mentioned them because I have not built any of their products or looked at them closely enough to give a fair assessment. However, I am not dismissing them. Reviews of their kits can be found on the websites that I describe in the next chapter.

Choosing your model

Faced with such a bewildering array of potential models from which to choose, making a rational decision might seem an impossible task, particularly if you are taking a first step into ship modelling from another genre. Let me offer some ideas for consideration, followed by a few specific suggestions.

You might well have in mind to build a model of a specific ship. This will narrow your choice, sometimes to a single kit. In such cases, be careful. Maybe you want to build *that ship*, but do you want to build *that kit*? If it is one of the 'classic' kits from the 1950s or the 1960s, you are immediately going to struggle to end up with a highly detailed and accurate replica. There are some people who relish

the challenge of making the sow's ear into a silk purse, but I'm not one of them. For myself, I look and see that there are so many good kits out there. Quite honestly, I would rather choose the silk purse to begin with.

This is where the local hobby shop can have an advantage; hopefully, you can open the kit to look at the parts. Maybe the owner would want to look over your shoulder, because many unscrupulous modellers might have opened a box just to steal a part that they have lost from the kit they are building. I would always have my doubts about buying an unknown kit from a dealer who refused to allow boxes to be opened.

12.

Tamiya's E-class destroyer. I am building this to represent HMS *Grenade*, because of an interesting colour scheme. The fo'c'sle will end up being slightly too long, but I am prepared to live with that, because trying to shorten it would lead to other problems.

13.

A company such as Tamiya has a generally good reputation for quality. But it started producing ships in the 1970s, and much of its list dates from that time. There are more modern kits that have come out in the past few years, so you may well want to look particularly at these much more detailed products, or those that have been re-tooled to supersede the older editions.

If you want to add photo-etch or replace details with after-market parts, you need to consider what the market can offer. Is there a dedicated set for the kit you are looking at, or if not, are there generic sets that can improve specific details? How much might these cost, and can you actually get them anywhere? Are you looking at a kit in an unusual scale for which no parts are produced? You might want to do some research before parting with your money.

If you are planning on trying out some of the techniques in this book, you might wish to consider a slightly less complex kit, with fewer parts. Don't misunderstand me, I am not trying to be patronising, it is just that a more straightforward kit offers a cleaner canvas on which to work.

13.

I built USS *Porter* about three years ago, and I'd happily do others in this line. This was the first model on which I used 'Caenis' fly-tying thread for the rigging.

The size and price of the model might well be an important factor. A large 1/350-scale ship may look very impressive but causes storage difficulties, especially if you want to put it in a cabinet or glass case. And if you are trying out new techniques, it makes sense to do it on something small, cheap and 'expendable', rather than the latest state-of-the-art *Takao* from Aoshima.

What about some specific suggestions for first ship modelling ventures? The following are purely personal recommendations, based on experience of certain manufacturers' kits, either by close examination or actually building them. If certain companies are missed, they should not feel automatically aggrieved, because I might well regard their products as more complex or exquisite, and suitable for modellers who have got a few kits under their belts.

For plastic kits, Tamiya is a good producer with which to start, and I would suggest one of its more recent offerings. The E-class British destroyer is a super little kit. It is sharply moulded and well detailed, although it could do with a bit of lifting in some areas, such as replacement of cable reels and watertight doors. There is also a dedicated photo-etched fret from White Ensign to go with it. With a little adjustment the kit could be used to represent a member of one of several classes of ships, with a correspondingly wide range of colour schemes and armament fits from which to choose.

If you wish to do something slightly bigger, you could look at Tamiya's USS *Indianapolis*, on which I demonstrate my techniques, with plenty of photo-etch to go with it, both dedicated and generic. There are plenty of pictures of the model later on.

Midway in terms of size between these two is a new release of the Japanese light cruiser *Abukuma*. This appears to be a striking improvement on Tamiya's original kits of such ships from the 1970s.

Don't be restricted to products from this one company. Trumpeter's *New Orleans*-class cruisers are new to the market and push the envelope in some aspects of detail, with moulded on 'eyebrows' or rain gutters over the scuttles. That is something you don't see every day.

For a first resin kit, I have often suggested to people trying one of Combrig's 1/700-scale US destroyers, such as the USS *Porter*, although I would choose one in a wartime fit. The prewar models feature tripod masts. These models are beautifully cast and go together easily with no construction issues. As with most resin kits, you have to provide your own railings, and the radars could do with replacement with finer photo-etch.

In a similar vein, you could look at one of the US destroyers from Niko, mentioned above. The detail is just as fine as, or even better than Combrig,

14.

I built *Starling* straight from the box. It was a nice relaxing project before I knuckled down to the task of writing this book!

14

but is very fragile. You might need to fill and re-drill the hull scuttles, which could be out of line.

White Ensign kits give everything you need, including photo-etch and railings, so you do not need to add anything else. I have made HMS *Starling*, but you could also choose either an L- or M-class destroyer. They are all available in 1/700 scale.

Samek kits are no longer in production, but they are sometimes to be found for sale at shows. Its 1/700-scale Tribal-class destroyers are smart, sharp and straightforward little things. HMS *Tartar* contains a photo-etched lattice mast that is convincing and interesting.

For cruiser-sized models, I heartily recommend

HMAS *Sydney* from NNT Modell. Built straight from the box, this will result in something very clean and attractive looking, although, as will be seen later, there is room for improvement, especially with regard to the bridge.

If you are new to ship modelling, and resin kits in particular, I would strongly advise you against getting ahead of yourself, and being too ambitious early on. There are hundreds of resin kits of battleships, aircraft carriers and heavy cruisers out there. Cut your teeth on a couple of smaller kits to begin with, such as those I have mentioned, and you will then be confident that you can do justice to the larger beauties.

CHAPTER 2
✑References and Resources✑

When I first began modelling, in the distant and sun-drenched land of my childhood, I was happy to take a kit, glue it together and then paint it without any worries about how precisely accurate it was. Most newcomers to the hobby would do the same and many long-time modellers would continue to do so.

There is absolutely nothing wrong with this. The most important criterion in our hobby is whether we are having fun doing it. It is that simple. I find it a refreshing break between large projects to take a small kit that I believe to be fairly complete and accurate and then put it all together with no more references than the diagrams in the instructions. It makes a change not to wake in the middle of the night worrying about the precise shade of blue I should be using or the date that a particular radar antenna was fitted.

Most of the time, however, I strive to be as accurate as possible, within reason. As modellers, we tend to reach a point where we begin asking ourselves just what that lump of plastic is supposed to represent, or we get suspicious that British, US, German and Japanese ships might not have used the same shade of Humbrol grey paint! At this time, we start to need more detailed sources of information, although we would make too much of it if we called ourselves researchers. Nevertheless, I should like to suggest some useful places to look.

15

⟨∽ *Books* ∽⟩

Particularly if we are interested in history as well as model-making, we tend to accumulate books on the areas or subjects that interest us. Of course, most general history books do not contain much of the technical information or the photos or plans that we really need to build accurate models. This sort of content is usually found in more 'peripheral' publications, and you may have to do a bit of searching for them. This is not to decry your local bookshop, because I have often found very interesting and useful naval books in my local branches of Waterstones and Borders.

I find a more useful hunting ground is a second-hand bookshop. I am lucky enough to live only twenty miles from McLaren Books in Helensburgh, near Glasgow. I have often spent happy mornings, not to mention numerous pounds, in this treasure house of maritime history.

If you are not so lucky, all is not lost, because you can easily browse catalogues online, and good booksellers do run mail order services. If you know the particular volume you are after, Internet sites such as <www.bookfinder.com>, <www.abebooks.com> and <www.alibris.com> can search a network of dealers worldwide to find available copies and compare prices. Some care is needed, because occasionally a seller may quote a ridiculously high price, and this is reckoned to be a way of ensuring a good return on investment in the event of an insurance claim. Although I have bought my share of expensive books, I have never been tempted to pay five times the going rate. But then again, I have never phoned such a dealer and asked what the *actual* best price on that book might be!

Bargains can still be found on these sites. A few years ago, I was lucky enough to find a copy of *British Cruisers of World War Two*, by Alan Raven

16.

___

This book dealer attends many of the major model shows in the UK. As usual, ships form a small part of her stock, but there is usually a selection of useful titles.

17.

___

Parkes, Burt and Raven & Roberts. Together, these books cost nearly £300. God bless my understanding wife!

15.

___

White Ensign's HMS *Starling*, built without any references. I trust the manufacturer enough to believe it is accurate, but if it isn't, I don't care! It was just a nice, fun build.

and John Roberts (usual price in excess of £100) listed for a mere £18, less than the cover price when new, some thirty years ago. It does not happen often.

Booksellers whose stock is most directly relevant to our hobby usually attend the larger regional or national model shows. Browsing their stands can be fruitful, and it may be possible to make a special order for some more obscure volume.

Let's look at some of the books on my shelves, or those that I think might be particularly useful.

Oscar Parkes, *British Battleships*. I have to mention this book because it really turned me on to warships. Rather old, delightfully partisan, and beautifully written. Perhaps not the most useful reference for a modeller, but it has pride of place on my shelf!

Alan Raven and John Roberts, *British Battleships of World War Two*. Companion volume to the volume on cruisers. Among the best books on the subject. Long out of print and commanding high prices on the second-hand market.

R A Burt, *British Battleships*. Three volumes covering from pre-dreadnoughts to the Second World War. Again extremely expensive.

Norman Friedman. Has written numerous books mainly concerned with US ship design. Technical, authoritative, but dry. Not really the best bedtime reading!

Warship. An annual publication consisting of well-researched articles on naval subjects, often of a technical or design nature. Past volumes are usually available from second-hand dealers.

'Conway's History of the Ship'. A multi-volume set dealing with the development of ships from the Stone Age to the present day. Very interesting background, although I do not find them very readable. Large number of illustrations and small comparative drawings.

M J Whitely. Volumes on battleships, cruisers and destroyers of the Second World War. Basic details of every class of these ships from every significant navy, including statistics, modifications and service histories. Not as authoritative as some books but useful background.

Roger Chesneau, *Aircraft Carriers of the World*. Identical format to the above volumes and the same comments apply.

'Ship Shape'. A series of monographs on specific types of ships. Of particular interest to us is the monograph on battlecruisers by John Roberts. Each volume contains a large-scale plan inside the back cover. Make sure that it has not been removed.

Stefan Terzibaschitsch, *Cruisers of the US Navy, 1922–1962*. Profusely illustrated book on a vast

---

18.

Whitely's book on destroyers and a volume from the Conway series.

19.

I have several of the 'Anatomy of the Ship' series. These two by Janusz Skulski are particularly good.

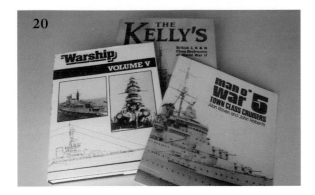

20.

21.

Some of the other books that I have found useful. I always try to pick up copies of *Warship* whenever I am in a second-hand book shop.

Some economically priced volumes. That does not mean they are poor quality. I refer to books such as these more often than most.

subject; unfortunately, some of the photographic reproduction is not very good.

'Anatomy of the Ship'. A series of books dealing with individual ships and consisting largely of comprehensive plans of every part of the ship. Most are highly regarded, although the volume on Bismarck is thought to be very disappointing.

This is just a selection of the larger books I own or would like to own. It is by no means comprehensive. For other books, you could do worse than to look out for those written by authors such as John Roberts, Andrew Raven, John Lambert, Alan Lambert, D K Brown, Antony Preston, and Al Ross.

For information on particular vessels or classes, smaller and sometimes less expensive series of books are often more useful.

Profile Publications. I remember these from my childhood. They can still be found on occasion, often bound together into hardback volumes. I suspect that scholarship has moved on since they were published. And you are not going to find them at the original price of one shilling and sixpence, or thereabouts!

Squadron/Signal Publications. Although this series

deals mainly with aircraft and armour, there are several naval titles. Excellent value and in a mainly pictorial format, there are some issues reported regarding accuracy, and the more recent volumes have some poor picture reproduction with pixelation.

'Ensign' and 'Man O'War'. Two sister series that only extended to a few volumes each. Long out of print, they are very expensive, perhaps too expensive for most people – full of information, though.

'Profile Morskie'. A Polish series of small volumes. Often very little text and bilingual photo captions, so an inability to read Polish is not a disadvantage. With a vast range of titles, the main advantage is the plans that these volumes contain. I understand that these plans are often used as references by model manufacturers. If these plans contain any inaccuracies they then become reproduced, and are then self-reinforcing as the modeller checks the kit against the plans. With this caveat, they are still very good value.

'Warship Perspectives'. A small series of slim volumes, each packed with information. Of particular use are the four volumes on Royal Navy camouflage in the Second World War, by Alan Raven. I believe there are some accuracy issues, but they are still the most useful references on this subject.

Magazines

Looking at the newsagents, I find that there are no widely available modelling magazines that are particularly useful for a ship modeller who is interested in kits. *Model Boats* and *Marine Modelling* seem to deal almost exclusively with large-scale, radio-control and plank-on-frame or other types of wooden construction. I used to regard *Fine Scale Modeler* as the best kit magazine on the market, and which was full of examples of inspiring work. Unfortunately, it has gone downhill and now offers more basic beginner's advice rather than the aspirational content it once had.

Other English language publications have come and gone, probably due to the Internet. *Plastic Ship Modeler* was defunct, or almost so, by the time I came to ship modelling. *Warship Modeler* was a quarterly that lasted for about two years. I found it bland and, in its kit reviews, unwilling to make a criticism, so that any complimentary comments could not be relied on either.

Other languages are better served by magazines that have either been around for a long time or built up quickly a good reputation. The French magazine *Navires et Histoire* has been around for years and seems to cover a wide range of maritime subjects over a long span of history. The Japanese series of magazines (although they could also be called monographs) that go under the titles of *Gakken* and *Model Art* seem to be mainly based on photographs of highly detailed models and deal almost exclusively with Japanese subjects. They have to be sought out. The Polish magazine *Modelarstwo Okretowe* began publication in 2006. It appears very impressive despite being only in the Polish language. It features plans, photos and striking computer-generated 3D graphics.

Internet resources

As mentioned above, I think that good monthly magazines for ship modellers are so thin on the ground because of the rise of the Internet. We are too small a segment of the hobby for paper periodicals to continue to make a profit. Their place has been taken by various websites, which perform some of the functions of the magazine just as well and others much better.

I would strongly encourage any new ship modeller to visit two websites – <www.modelwarships.com> and <www.steelnavy.com> – and do so regularly, maybe even on a daily basis.

Both sites post reviews of new kits and accessories, have galleries in which members can post photos of their models and forums in which members can discuss subjects related to modelling, naval history and technology and sometimes entirely unrelated topics. If you join in the discussions, and begin to ask questions, you will find the other members extremely helpful and friendly. Do not be afraid of sounding stupid in the questions you ask, because someone is bound to reassure you that the only really stupid question is the one not asked! Sometimes the discussions can get heated, especially if the subject is the colour of USS *Arizona* on the morning of 7 December 1941.

The kit reviews are more thorough than most of those found in magazines and there are far more of them. It is possible to get a much fuller idea of the relative quality of different manufacturers, which is very useful at the time to make your own choices.

Take the plunge and post your own images. You will find that models of all standards are exhibited in the galleries. You will get only encouragement. You will also see very fine examples of modelling, and if you ask about the techniques used, most people will be only too happy to share them with you.

Modelling has a reputation for being a hobby for loners. The Internet means that it no longer has to be like that. I have made friends through these sites, and you may be reassured that, unlike teenage social networking sites, there is nothing remotely dubious or suspicious about them.

Other useful forum-based sites are the *Ship Modeller's Mailing List*, which is now based on Yahoo!, and <www.modelshipwrights.com>.

The Internet is home to several image archives. I list just a few.

www.navsource.org A vast collection of images of US Navy ships from the late nineteenth century to the present day.

www.navyphotos.co.uk   A private collection of images of Royal Navy ships that has been opened up for view.

www.cyber-heritage.co.uk   An enormous site containing thousands and thousands of images, mainly to do with Plymouth. Hidden in its midst are some sections to do with Royal Navy ships of the nineteenth and twentieth centuries.

www.navweaps.com Naval weapons of most major nations. Mostly specifications and dimensions, but a small number of images.

www.dockmuseum.co.uk   Home to the Vickers photographic archive, where you will find Vickers' official images of the guns and some of the ships it built at Barrow in Furness.

www.tsushima.org A Russian language site that is not as good as it once was. Images of Russian, British, French and US ships. Difficult to navigate and slow to download.

www.shipcamouflage.com A very useful site that features details of camouflage schemes for British and US ships. It contains a forum but at the time of writing this is not operational.

www.servicehistorique.sga.defense.gouv.fr   The French government has had a vast number of its warship plans available to the public free of charge. Be prepared to spend some time trawling through the list to find what you want, because the files do not have good descriptions of their contents.

www.francois.delboca.free.fr A site entitled *Dates Marquantes et Anecdotes du Port de La Rochelle-Pallice*. It contains a large collection of French warship images, mainly from old postcards.

When you find a good image archive site that appears not to be an offshoot of an official organisation, it might be a good idea to download or print off as much of the information as possible, computer memory allowing. Websites have a tendency to be transient entities and content might not be available to you indefinitely. For example, the Tsushima site, mentioned above, seems to have lost the majority of its images, and another wonderful site called something like 'Ariga's Photo Site', has completely disappeared into the digital æther, along with thousands of images, especially of British ironclads and pre-dreadnoughts. 'Oh, woe is me!'

∽ *Museums* ∾

If you are lucky enough to live close to a good maritime museum you might have a valuable resource in terms of the models in its collection. If you are a Londoner, the National Maritime Museum, Chatham Dockyard and the Imperial War Museum will be important places to visit with a camera. I live in Glasgow and I count myself fortunate to be able to go to the Museum of Transport, which has probably the best collection of builders' models in the country. Although this type of model is extremely detailed, you must remember that these were intended to represent the ship as it was planned, not necessarily its appearance as it was completed or while in service. Close examination of models such as these can give valuable insights into shapes of fittings and other structures.

At the risk of being a pest to the wife or girlfriend, take every opportunity to visit and go aboard preserved or museum ships. This is where digital photography is so good. You can take photos without limit, and not have to worry about the cost of developing. You may have no wish to make a model of the particular ship you are on, but observing and photographing details and fittings will give valuable information about similar items on ships that do interest you. Once again, be aware that museum ships usually represent the ship at the end of its service life, and there may have been significant changes in its appearance from the most interesting period in it history. For example, HMS *Belfast* is very much changed from its wartime configuration, having a lattice mast and Hazemeyer Bofors guns, but no pom-pom guns or catapult. It also sports a totally spurious camouflage scheme.

22.

A builder's model of a *King Edward VII*-class battleship. Models such as these can be invaluable for clarifying areas that might be difficult to elucidate on plans. The boat stowage arrangements on ships such as these have always been a bit of a mystery to me, and I believe they have frequently been wrongly represented.

23.

The bridge of HMS *Cavalier* at Chatham. Use images to give inspiration for the clutter of equipment in areas such as this.

⁓*Model Shows*⁓

Wherever you live, in most of the UK at least, you will find that there is a model show relatively close to you at some time during the year. Time spent at most such shows would not be wasted. They are not just opportunities to buy kits at bargain prices but, more importantly, you are able to carefully examine the completed models on the tables and to discuss them with other modellers. And do not be ashamed to enter the competitions. Maybe you will not win anything, but that really does not matter. The best mental attitude to have is to realise that people look most closely at the models that are in the competitions, and by entering yours, it is the best way to get people to look at your own handiwork. And do not be surprised, you may win a medal!

Try to visit the national shows, such as the British IPMS Show at Telford every November. This is regarded as the largest model show in the world, and although it has a different format, I believe that it is even larger than the American IPMS Nationals. It attracts visitors from all over the UK and Europe; from Norway to Malta, from the Canaries to Poland. Here you will see the finest examples of contemporary kit modelling, and be able to chat with the foremost experts in the hobby, most of whom will be happy to give advice and suggestions. If you are active on the websites, you may already have made their acquaintance. It is then great to meet them face to face. You would be assured of a warm welcome. It is always one of the most important dates on my calendar and I hope it will also be on yours.

24

24.

I took several photos of this Nordenfeldt machine gun on board HMS *Gannet* at Chatham. I do not have any immediate use for them, but one never knows what is going to come in useful in the future.

CHAPTER 3
ᴄ⊃Tools, Techniques and Materialsᴄ⊃

In talking about choice of tools, I assume you already have a toolkit, and that you know about sanding sticks, needle files, pin chucks and the like. But I would like to make a few comments about certain choices you could make with regard to basic tools if you are shopping for them.

ᴄ⊃Hand Toolsᴄ⊃

I am a great enthusiast for proper surgical scalpel blades, of the type made by Swann-Morton. I have tried using the craft-knife type blades made by X-Acto but cannot get on with them. Although the blades are initially very sharp, the steel from which they are made is extremely brittle and the points fragile. They do not stand up to heavy usage, such as trying to cut photo-etch or metal shim. Scalpel-blade steel is much tougher and a far better choice.

Scalpel blades and handles are readily available from craft shops, but if you have a good relationship with the pharmacist in your local chemist's shop, it might be possible to order them in a bulk box of 100, which would save a tidy sum of money.

You will do well to have several pairs of tweezers, in various shapes and sizes. It is tempting to get the finest available, on the grounds that you will be doing delicate, miniature work. However, fine points have a tendency to bend and get out of true so that they do not grip well. I find that my most reliable tweezers are actually a more robust pair. The most important thing is to ensure that they have jaws that close absolutely parallel, because it is most frustrating being unable to grab hold of a wayward rigging fibre.

Last year, I picked up a new razor saw, which has interchangeable and multiple blades with spacers. This enables you to make parallel cuts and you can therefore produce identically shaped blocks

25.

Some of my favourite hand tools.

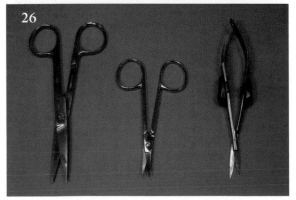

26.

At left, a pair of surgical scissors, robust and good for general use. At centre, a pair of fine scissors, intended for embroidery, but far too good for the wife to use! At right, a pair of spring scissors, bought from the angling shop and meant for fly-tying. I use these for rigging.

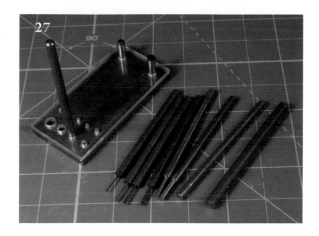

27.

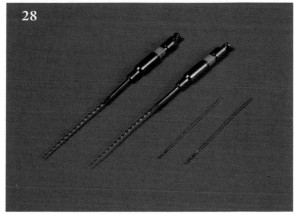

28.

I find this punch very useful for producing discs of plastic, the sort of thing needed for small platforms or for plating over hull scuttles on wartime ships. But it is a device that looks as though it has been produced by hand in small numbers, and it is extremely expensive for what it is.

by using this saw on a strip of plastic. Ammunition lockers can be exactly the same size.

∽ *Power tools* ∽

Many modellers have a high-speed miniature drill, such as a Dremel. They can be used with a variety of different bits, such as drills, cutters, saws, wire brushes and polishers. I do not use mine a great deal, because I find that the speed at which it rotates is so fast that the heat produced would easily melt polystyrene plastic and clog the blades of the cutter. This is not an issue with resin, and the Dremel can be used with alacrity to carve away, doing such things as hollowing funnels and boats or removing the underwater portions of hulls. The major problem is vast amounts of dust, and use of a mask is advisable. I think it is a great pity that these drills rotate at such high speeds, because they might be much more useful if their minimum was a lot slower than 5,000 or 10,000rpm.

A couple of years ago, I discovered some wonderful drills that are excellent for use in a Dremel. They are dental root-canal drills. They come in diameters as fine as 0.15mm, and are flexible so they will not break as readily as ordinary twist drills. They are perfect for drilling a hole to take something as fine as rigging fibre, and if you do not want a hole that is too visible, and would need filling.

The airbrush

Airbrushes are regarded as a normal part of the modeller's toolkit, and many would not be without them. I am one of those, but some extremely good modellers never use them, and produce stunning work by just hand brushing. Although I can cope with putting the paints on by hand, for applying coats of protective or matt varnish, I find that an airbrush is the only tool to use.

Aircraft and armour modellers will need to apply finishes that have mottled or soft edged designs. They will find that expensive and sophisticated double-action airbrushes are advantageous. Ship modellers are unlikely to want to do that, as ships tend to have hard-edged designs requiring masking. Most ship modellers could get away with a much simpler, single-action brush. If you are spraying up to a piece of masking tape, the ability to paint a fine line 2mm wide is not necessary. However, the higher range models are easier to use and easier to keep clean. The most expensive airbrushes on the market are probably not going to be a good choice for modellers.

Intended for use by professional illustrators, they have nozzles that are designed to spray special inks. They will not perform optimally with paints, which have solid grains of pigment.

If you are planning on doing a lot of airbrushing, give careful consideration to how you will power it. Although cans of propellant are readily available, the cost of continually buying these will soon mount up, and in the long run a proper compressor would be cheaper, despite the initial outlay. Canned propellants last for only a short time and have a habit of running out at the most awkward times, such as right in the middle of a job. The last thing you want is to be left holding an airbrush that is full of paint, which will soon solidify, and with no way to clean it out.

Other power tools

Apart from a small soldering iron, and occasionally stealing my wife's hairdryer in order to dry paint quickly, I do not use any other power tools on a regular basis. I do not own a lathe or circular saw. I do have an electric jigsaw and a disc sander under the bench, but I cannot remember the last time I switched either of them on. It might be an entirely different thing if I was making scratch-built models, but for working on kits, I have found no use for anything else. It's simple as that.

∽ *Paintbrushes* ∽

Even if you are using an airbrush for the larger areas of painting, you will end up doing a lot of painting by hand. In choosing paintbrushes, the most fundamental question to ask is whether to go for natural hair or synthetic. It is not the case that the most expensive brushes are necessarily the best – not for modellers' purposes, at least. Although I have several very costly Kolinsky sable brushes, which are unbeatable for painting model soldiers in artist's oils, I find that less expensive synthetic brushes perform better with acrylic paints. Sable brushes are very good for oil-based enamel paints, but tend to splay their hairs out and lose their points with acrylic paint, especially if it has been thinned with water. I suspect it is something to do with the high surface tension of water. It is also

much less annoying to have to throw out a cheap £4 synthetic brush than a £15 sable brush because you have forgotten to wash it out!

Synthetic brushes perform well with any kind of paint, especially the larger sized and flat brushes. They stand up to hard use and abuse, and can cope with cleaning with powerful solvents such as acetone. With some brands, however, the ends of the hairs have a habit of bending over with use, and the precise, springy point is lost, making detailed painting difficult.

My general suggestions for paintbrush choice would be:

Large flat areas: Synthetic flat brushes, in sizes from 3/16in up.
General painting: Round brushes in various sizes. Mostly synthetic but get a couple of sables if you are feeling wealthy or extravagant.
Fine details:- Some small sables, but don't abuse them. You might occasionally find some specialized synthetic brushes that are useful. Try to get a couple of really tiny brushes, sizes 00 or 000 – maybe even 0000 if you can find them.

29.

At left, expensive sable brushes, Winsor & Newton, Series 7. At centre, synthetic brushes of various shapes. At right, small synthetic brushes; useful for tiny details.

29

ᴄᴏ *Some basic techniques* ᴄᴏ

There are a few techniques that are fundamental to good ship modelling but different from the handling of the plastic or resin. They will crop up all the way through the building process, so I think it is best if show you these separately here. I hope this will explain these more clearly than trying to do it piecemeal in the coming pages.

Handling metal

I use photo-etched metal in all of my models. It might just be railings, but more often a large number of parts will be added, improved or replaced in this medium. On the model of USS *Indianapolis*, I shall also replace the splinter shields with fine brass sheet. Cutting, bending and handling metal parts, often incredibly delicate, are crucial skills to master.

31.

Thin brass shim, about 2 thou in thickness, is easy to cut using a scalpel blade. Using the tile once again, position the ruler precisely and hold it very firmly. This time use a pointed scalpel blade, and make several gentle passes along the cutting line. You will not cut through the brass in one pass, but after about three or four, you should feel the sensation of the blade going through the other side. I also suggest beginning and ending the cut a little short of both edges of the sheet of brass. This will keep both ends of the strip under control and prevent distortion.

Cutting brass in this fashion will raise a sharp burr on the edge, which would usually need to be removed. Hold the strip flat on the tile and make a couple of firm passes down it with a fine sanding stick. This will remove the burr in most cases.

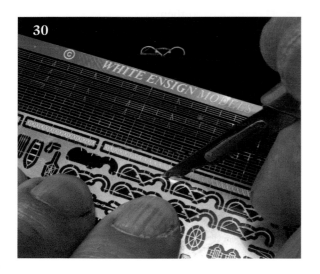

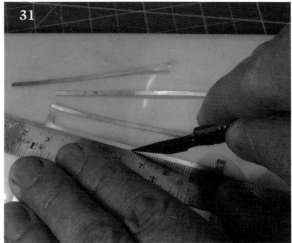

30.

Metal, such as photo-etch, is cut on a hard surface. I use a ceramic wall tile but a piece of thick glass will do as well. Take a new scalpel blade, preferably a proper Swann-Morton blade with a curved edge, and cut through the attachment points by pressing down vertically. Do not use a sawing motion, especially on railings or other delicate parts, because this is very likely to distort the brass. Small parts have an annoying tendency to 'ping' off the table and be lost in the carpet, so be careful. If there is any roughness left at the point of the cut, hold the part in square nosed pliers and give a stroke or two with a fine file or sanding stick.

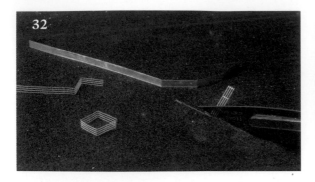

32.

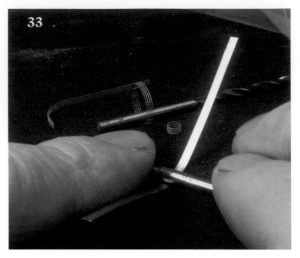

33

While cutting brass is best done on a hard surface, simple bends are best accomplished using a softer, resilient surface. I would recommend the back of a computer mouse mat, preferably a cheap and thin example, rather than a more luxurious type. The sort of thing given away by sales reps for advertising is ideal. I always bend railings like this. With the railing on the back of the mat, press straight down with a straight scalpel blade and both ends will bend up, giving a sharp corner. You can achieve multiple bends to makes squares, rectangles or 'Z' shapes. Brass strips can be bent in exactly the same way. It is important to ensure that the blade crosses the railing exactly at a right angle, otherwise the resulting structure will be horribly squint.

Curves are easy on a mouse mat. Take a round object, brass rod, a file handle or the shank of a drill and roll it along the length of the railing or strip pressing down as you do. A progressive curving of the metal will result. The pressure you exert and the diameter of the rod can determine the radius. It is even possible to end up with a complete and exact circle. This is the sort of thing you will want if you are making a gun tub or putting railings around a searchlight platform.

34.

For complex photo-etched components, requiring multiple bends, a proprietary bending tool is a useful investment. The two major brands are 'Hold & Fold' and 'Etch Mate'. There is not much to choose between them. They both consist of a spring-loaded clamp that holds the photo-etch firmly against a straight edge. The bend is then made by lifting with a razor blade. Where the fold is long, this is a more reliable method than the mouse mat. If I used this special tool for nothing else, I would still want it for bending up the handrails on inclined ladders.

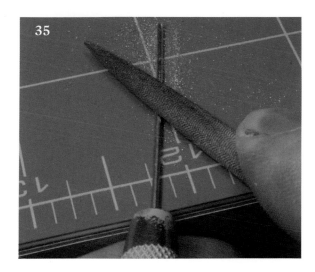

35.

It is not necessary to purchase specially made tapered brass masts for your ship. Nor do you need to have a lathe to make them yourself. All I do is put a length of brass rod of suitable diameter into a pin chuck, and holding it so that the rod is flat on the work-bench, go at it with a file. I turn the pin chuck with my left hand to ensure that all sides of the rod are filed, and make strokes of different lengths, so that I take off more at the end of the rod that is to be narrow. When I have finished, I smooth things down with wet and dry paper. It takes only a few minutes to make a mast for a 1/700 ship.

Soldering

Metal to metal joints can be made with glue, either cyanoacrylate or two-part epoxy, but if the joint is to be subject to any kind of stress, such as with a fully rigged mast, you cannot beat soldering. I am no expert, but I can achieve simple joints. Basic equipment is all that is needed: a 15W soldering iron, some solder, liquid flux, fine wet and dry paper and a way of holding the parts in position.

When I soldered the mainmast tripod for *Indianapolis*, I had the three legs with solder applied standing in a jig. The soldering iron was applied to the top of the tripod to fuse the joint. When I took it away, a small peak of solder appeared at the joint, such as when removing a spoon from whipped cream, and this needed to be filed off.

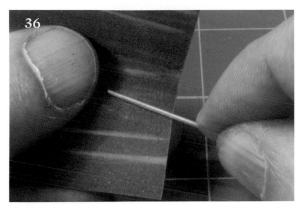

36.

Solder bonds to metal but not to the layer of oxide that soon forms on it. Absolute cleanliness is a prerequisite for success. Immediately before attempting to solder, the mating surfaces must be rubbed with wet and dry paper to make them shiny. Do not touch them with greasy fingers after that.

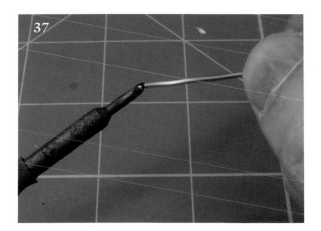

37.

Before switching on the soldering iron, file the bit to reveal shiny copper. When it has heated up enough, apply a small amount of solder to the bit; enough to cover the surface of the bit but not enough to make a big molten blob. This is called 'tinning' the bit. If there is a large amount of molten solder, wipe or flick it off. The iron will be used to transfer solder to the metal pieces. What you will not be doing is heating the joint between the metal pieces and attempting to get solder to run into the gap.

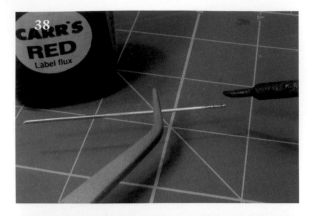

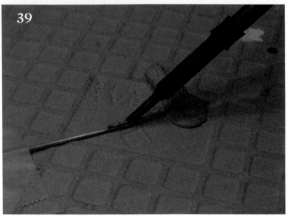

38.

Hold the piece of brass in tweezers or pliers, or secure it to the work surface; don't hold it with your fingers! Brush a drop of flux over the mating surface. Take the tinned soldering iron and simply stroke the bit along the area of the joint. A film of solder will transfer to the brass. Do the same thing for both joint surfaces.

39.

Devise a suitable way of holding both parts in the correct position with the mating surfaces touching. I use Blu-Tack or masking tape on the back of a ceramic tile. Ensure that everything is exactly straight and in line, because you will be unable to adjust things afterwards without breaking the joint. Apply another drop of flux to the joint. Take the hot soldering iron and wipe the bit on a thick cloth to remove all but a trace of solder. Touch the iron onto one of the metal parts, close to the joint, taking care not to disturb the alignment. Almost instantly, the heat passes through the metal to the joint, where the solder melts and flows between the brass parts. Note that you are not putting the soldering iron into the joint itself in an attempt to melt the solder directly. Remove the iron and the solder immediately solidifies, resulting in a rigid joint that is much stronger than glue. You might have to do a little cleaning up with a file or sanding stick if a bit too much solder has been deposited.

Resin casting

Using polyurethane resin to cast parts or to copy those included in kits is a useful skill to acquire, although it could be a bit messy and the materials could be on the pricey side.

Some people would take the view that it is immoral or dishonest to make copies from parts in commercially available kits. I respect their opinion but would make a couple of observations.

First, resin manufacturers will often use commercially available parts, such as photo-etched doors and hatches in their master models, which they then cast from in order to make their kits, which are sold to us. This seems to be regarded as quite acceptable practice, although it is totally different from making a straight copy of someone else's complete product and passing it off as your own – a disreputable practice that does sometimes happen.

My personal opinion is that it is reasonable to make copies of parts from kits provided certain conditions are met: I must have bought the original kit with my own money; I am only going to copy some parts, not the whole kit; I am doing it for my own use and not intending to sell the copies to anyone else; And, finally, the maker of the kit is not selling the parts separately as an accessory. If all these are fulfilled, my conscience is clear.

The materials you will need consist of two-part mould rubber compound, two-part casting resin, mould release spray, mixing containers, a few syringes for measuring, stirring sticks, and cardboard or plastic card for building the mould.

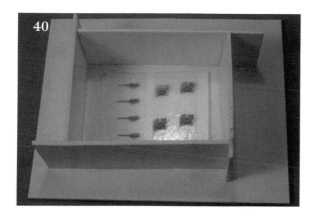

40.

41.

Build a simple box in which to make the mould. You can use either cardboard or plastic card, but it is easier to get good joins without leaks by using plastic. Do not make it any larger than you have to, because that would just waste the expensive silicone rubber mould compound. It should be sufficient for this to be about 1cm larger all round than the part that you are copying and 1cm deeper than its maximum height. By multiplying the length, breadth and depth of the mould you can work out how much mould rubber to mix. A slightly smaller piece of plastic card in the bottom of the mould will ensure that when the open-faced mould is inverted, there is a lip to stop casting resin from running everywhere. The parts to be copied are held in position with double-sided tape. In this case they are 5in anti-aircraft guns and mountings from Combrig's USS *Astoria*.

The plastic box has been broken away and the original parts removed from the rubber mould to leave true impressions. If there has been some creep of the mould rubber, causing partial flashing over of the voids, trim carefully with scissors in order to make it easier to fill the mould with resin.

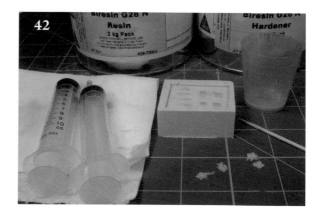

42.

It is now necessary to fill the box with silicone rubber to make a female mould of the items you wish to cast. Prepare enough of the mould rubber compound to fill the box. Measure out the proportions very carefully to get a correct cure. Mix very thoroughly but slowly to minimise the number of air bubbles in the mixture. Spray some mould release into the mould box to stop the rubber sticking too much. Brush a layer of the mixture over the parts in the box, getting it into all the nooks and crannies. Use an old brush. This is to prevent air bubbles being left in contact with the parts. Pour the rest of the mould rubber carefully into the box and set it aside to cure for 24 hours.

Spray the mould with releasing agent. Mix up equal volumes of the casting resin and hardener, or whatever the instructions tell you. Use a flexible pot and only make as much as you need to fill the mould once, because it begins setting straight away; anything not poured immediately is wasted. Work quickly to mix thoroughly and then pour. I squeeze the mould and use a cocktail stick to winkle out air bubbles and to ensure that the mould is completely filled with resin. After about 15 minutes, the resin will be solid and the castings can be extracted.

43.

Not all of the cast parts will be perfect. Some will show that the mould was not fully filled. Some will have voids from air bubbles trapped in the casting process. Others will have round balls attached if an air bubble is retained in the rubber while the original mould was curing. I reckon on producing three times as many parts as I actually need in order to get enough good parts.

Glues and fillers

Before we leave this area, let me explain something about the various glues and fillers that I shall be using.

Polystyrene cement
I only use liquid cement, and the thinner the better. Something like Humbrol Liquid Poly is ideal. I do not like the Revell Contacta glue in the squeezy bottle with the steel nozzle, although it does appear to give very strong joints. I cannot remember the last time I ever bought an old-fashioned tube of polystyrene cement, but it must have been more than 30 years ago.

Epoxy resin
Two-part epoxy is more useful in resin kits, but also has a role in plastic kits, for gluing metal, either to itself or to plastic. It does not have the instant bond of cyanoacrylate, but that is an advantage if a bit of 'wiggle time' is needed to get things positioned perfectly. It is also more reliable than cyanoacrylate if a joint is critical and subject to some stress, such as on a mast with a lot of rigging attached. Please, trust me on this!! The fast setting type is more useful, but I think that the old type that takes 24 hours to cure is stronger.

Cyanoacrylate (CA)
Both thin and thick CA, commonly called superglue, are good for sticking resin and metal to themselves, to each other or to plastic. They are even better for sticking important pieces to your fingers! They are, however, temperamental glues

and the thin type requires you to get parts exactly positioned before application. The CA joints can also be remarkably weak under some circumstances and I suggest that you do not use it for attaching railings.

Polyvinyl acetate (PVA)
Polyvinyl acetate is widely available in many different brands of white glue for wood or paper, and it is all basically the same stuff. It is surprisingly useful for non-critical joints, for example building up constructions in photo-etch. It can be diluted with water for brush application. It can be used for filling a fine joint line where normal filler might force you to sand away detail. I'd also advise you to use it for fixing railings, especially if your models are going to be exposed to extremes of temperature.

A similar type of glue is sold under the name of Gator Glue. I have not had much experience of it but it is has some good reports.

Stationer's gum
Do you remember the old-fashioned amber coloured stuff they gave us in school for sticking paper, in the bottle with the squidgy rubber cap? This is wonderful stuff if you can find it. Unfortunately, people have gone over to using glue sticks and it is no longer on the stationer's shelves. But you can get it on special order, although you may need to get a wholesale quantity. A litre bottle is currently about £8, so that is quite possibly a price that you will be willing to pay. At Chapter 9,

on rigging, you will find out why I love this liquid gold so much.

Fillers

Filling gaps and seam lines is a basic process in building any model kit. If you enter a model in a competition, a visible seam line is among the first faults that the judges will look for and they will mark you down because of it.

The commonest types of filler are those produced by Humbrol, Revell, and Squadron. These have a toluene-based solvent that is volatile and evaporates quickly, causing the filler to harden. The solvent also allows the filler to bond to polystyrene plastic, giving a solid joint. I currently use Squadron Green putty. I find that this hardens much more quickly than other brands and is ready for filing or sanding in only one hour.

Two-part-epoxy fillers such as Milliput are good for situations in which a hard compound is required, for example if it needs to be carved or drilled, or if a component is being built up. These fillers have to be kneaded to mix together the two components. Milliput tends to be rather sticky, and I find it makes a mess of my fingers. Andrea Sculp is softer and kneads more easily. Although expensive, it can be mixed in very small amounts.

Both these fillers can be smoothed with water to ease the shaping process. I would tend to use one of these if I had a crooked line of scuttles along a hull, and wanted to fill them before re-drilling.

Car body fillers, such as Plastic Padding or Isopon, are excellent for working quickly, with the least interruption while waiting for things to go solid. A compound such as this can be useful if a large area needs to be covered thickly, or if great depth is required. Mixed properly, it goes hard and is ready for sanding in only five minutes, so that you have to work swiftly, with confidence and panache, otherwise the filler will be going off before you finish applying it to your model!

Some modellers have used lateral thinking to come up with novel and unusual ways of filling seams on models. PVA glue can be painted into a seam, and excess removed with a damp tissue before it dries. Thick CA glue, applied over a seam and sprayed with accelerator, gives an instant and very hard joint. It is actually harder than the plastic or resin, so that can be a disadvantage if you need to sand it down. Tipp-Ex correction fluid is recommended by some people.

Now, if you're still with me, let's get on to the interesting bits. Let's make a model or two!

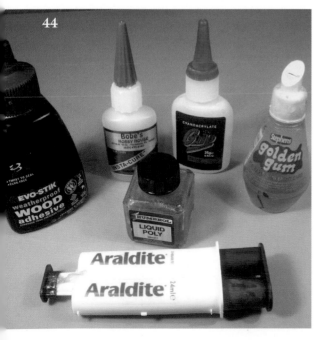

44.

Back row, left to right: PVA glue, thin CA, thick CA, Stationer's gum. Centre: Liquid polystyrene cement. Front: Epoxy resin.

45.

A variety of different fillers.

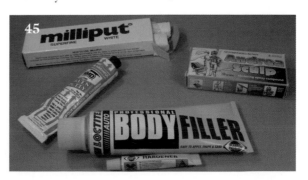

CHAPTER 4
ᕦBasic Construction: Plastic Modelsᕤ

In this chapter, I take you through the sequence of improving, detailing and putting together the major components of a typical injection-moulded kit. For clarity of explanation, processes such as using photo-etch and after-market resin parts, painting and weathering are dealt with separately in subsequent chapters, although, in reality, all of these processes will be occurring at the same time in the actual construction of a model.

The subject I have chosen is the Tamiya 1/700-scale model of the heavy cruiser USS *Indianapolis*. This is a high-standard kit that has been on the market since about 2000. In typical Tamiya fashion, the detailing is fine and restrained and not in the least bit toy-like. It does not suffer from sloping vertical surfaces, like some manufacturers' products, but as a result of the limitations of injection moulding, some surfaces have no detail at all, and have scope for its addition. Most of the splinter shields and bulwarks are admirably thin and, if we are honest, only need a little scraping to make them finer. However, I shall remove most of them to show how they can be replaced with brass sheet for an even better scale appearance. The completed model won a bronze medal at the American IPMS Nationals in 2008.

The main references that I shall use for the model are the Classic Warships publication on *Indianapolis* and the Squadron/Signal publication *US Heavy Cruisers*.

The 40mm Bofors guns provided are better than most that are found in 1/700 plastic kits. However, I shall be replacing these with stunning resin parts from Niko. The heavy anti-aircraft guns will also be replaced by making resin copies from a Combrig kit that is in my stash.

I will do a bit of scratch-building to replace the kit parts for the mainmast, because injection moulded masts are usually too thick, and this is one part of the kit that certainly does lack appropriate detail.

∞ *Planning the work* ∞

An explanation of the construction sequence and reasons for it will be useful.

Almost all ship kits would benefit from being broken down into a number of sub-assemblies, which are built and painted in their entirety before these are brought together later for final assembly. Warships are complex structures, with decks above other decks, and gun mountings, boats, lockers, etc., occupying much of the horizontal space. If construction gets too advanced, you might well find that while painting, some areas are inaccessible to the brush, due to overhanging decks or other projections.

Think ahead. Study the kit. Look at the instructions, but do not feel that they have to be followed in exact sequence. They are not written

46.

47.

This model was among the first of the new generation of ship kits. The hull parts for the kit show sharp scuttles and a very precise representation of the armour belt as well as pipelines for what I assume is aviation fuel.

As with the hull, Tamiya has done a creditable job with the detail of the smaller parts. The only thing that I'd really want to quibble about is the splinter shields for the Bofors and Oerlikon positions on the forward deckhouse (upper right). These are far too shallow and need correcting.

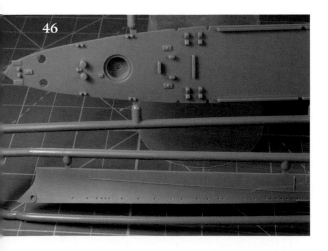

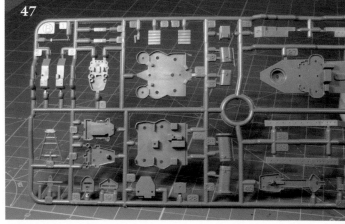

48.

The main photo-etch fret that I shall be using is the specific *Indianapolis* set by White Ensign. This includes almost everything that would be necessary to dress up the model, including floater net baskets. These are obvious on photos of US ships of the Second World War, but often omitted from models. Although this set contains railings, I use the ultra-fine railings by Gold Medal, which I consider to be the best on the market.

with the needs of painting in mind. They are written so that a complete novice can get every part in the right place. The fact that you are reading this book shows that you are far beyond that stage. Try and predict any pitfalls in the kit. Then devise your plan of attack.

In building *Indianapolis*, I shall make the whole of the hull, plus the lowest level of the forward superstructure, the after 5in gun deck and the stern 40mm gun tub into one sub-assembly. Getting this far in fitting things together allows the maximum number of joint lines to be dealt with, filled and hidden before painting, and there is nothing in this large structure that is going to impede this.

In contrast, each platform of the bridge above this lowest level needs to be done separately; built, painted, with small fittings being added and then finally brought together on top of each other, like the tiers of a wedding cake. Photo-etched ladders and similar twiddly bits are added in as we go.

After this, smaller completed units such as secondary guns, masts, radars, boats, catapults, etc., are added. I then add railings that have not already been fitted, working from the centreline out towards the sides of the ship. Rigging is almost the last major thing to be done, partly because it is delicate and easily damaged and because the railings are used to secure a lot of it.

That said, the sequence is not written in stone, and many deviations may be needed, which you will discover when you are building your own ships.

Now, let's get building!

⌒*The hull*⌒

There is no logical reason why one should have to start construction with the hull, if it is going to be done in sub-assemblies. But it is necessary to start somewhere, and the hull gets us off to an enthusiastic start.

The hull sides of the kit show impressive detailing of the armour belt, fuel lines and some fine and shallow scuttles (portholes to the uninitiated). I did not want to lose any of this. There are boat booms moulded onto the hull side, and I trimmed these off because I replaced them with plastic rod later on to get a less solid appearance. Location holes for the propeller guards needed to be filled because the photo-etch replacements did not need them.

The hull has rows of scuttles represented by shallow circular depressions. These do very well for a scuttle with the interior cover closed, but in harbour at least, a few would be open and it is possible to simulate this by drilling them a bit deeper. I took a 0.6mm drill in my pin chuck and took a few turns in each scuttle that I wanted to open, the same number of turns in each to ensure an even depth of drilling. A small amount of dust or swarf was left in the hole after the drill was removed. The easiest way that I have found to deal with this is to put the drill into the pin chuck the wrong way round, so that the shank is sticking out rather than the cutting end. I pushed this carefully but firmly into each hole that I had drilled and any debris was rammed down out of the way and lost to sight.

49.

When I glued the black base to the hull, an ugly seam line resulted. This needed to be filled and then sanded with great care to protect the hull side detail. I have no great preference for any particular brand of model filler, but find that Squadron Green dries very fast and enables me to trim, scrape and sand after only one hour. In order to get a smooth finish, I use foam-backed sanding sticks, either bought from a hobby supplier or from the manicure stand at the local chemist. I reckon they are basically the same thing. Using these with water, and going down in grit from the coarser to the very finest, it is possible to get an almost mirror-like finish.

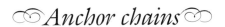

Anchor chains

The forecastle deck has the anchor chains moulded in place. Although Tamiya has managed to produce these more finely than most other manufacturers, I decided to remove and replace them with something that has an even better scale appearance. It is a frequently asked question on the modelling forums, 'Where can I get chain fine enough for the model that I am making?' It is possible to get very fine chain from model railway suppliers or from jewellers, but even the very finest that is made is still, in my opinion, far too heavy for any 1/700 model, even a battleship, although it might do for a 1/350 or larger model. Photo-etched chain can be found in very fine gauges, if you are lucky, but is flat and unconvincing.

For this model, I made replacement chains by braiding fine copper wire of 0.08mm diameter, from hi-fi speaker cable, into a simple three-strand plait. If you want to convince people that you are a real salty sea dog, you will use the term sinnet rather than plait!

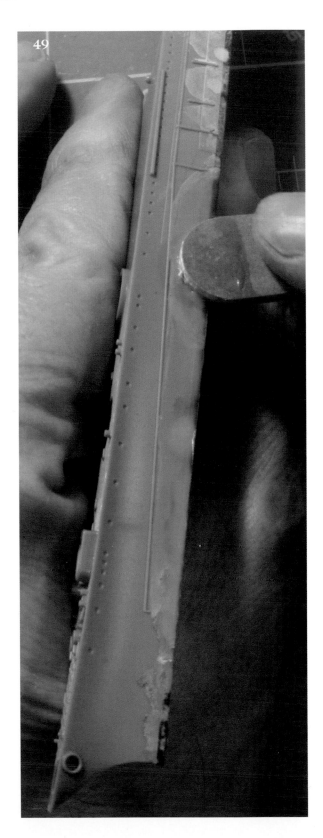

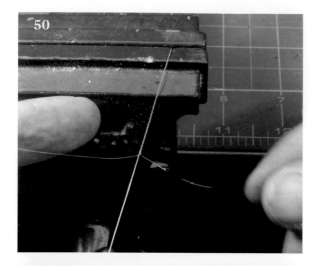

50.

Three lengths of wire were knotted together and the end secured in a vice. Alternately the left and right wires were passed over the middle wire, in exactly the same way that a girl would plait her hair into a pigtail. If you do not know the sequence, ask any woman of your acquaintance. I moved each wire sharply out to the side as its turn came, and kept a gentle tension on whichever wire was the current middle wire. Working rhythmically, it took me only ten minutes to plait the few inches needed for this model.

51.

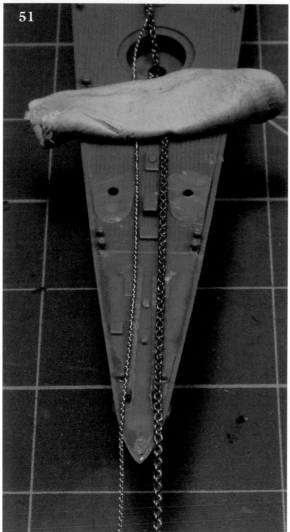

Here we see the plaited wire compared to the finest chain that I have been able to find. The chain would probably be suitable for a model of 1/350 scale, but it is far too big for this model. Although the plait that I have made is not an actual chain, the visual appearance is much better, and that is what counts. For a battleship in 1/700, I would still use plaited wire but choose something slightly thicker to work with. If you turn to the chapter on resin kit construction, you will find that I describe how to braid a 'four strand square sinnet'. This gives a more three dimensional impression to the imitation chain.

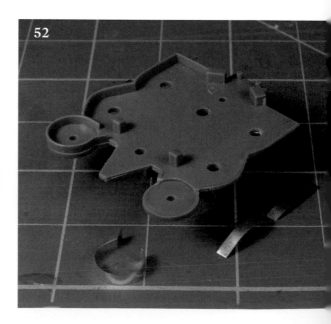

∽*Splinter shields*∽

An American ship such as this has splinter shields of thin armour plate around every gun position and every platform of the bridge. On most plastic models, these are fairly unconvincing. On kits from the 1970s and the 1980s, the shields are often just a thick and shallow rim to the platform, and look more like a box hedge in the garden of a chateau. Others show the 'sloping vertical' phenomenon, in which they are thicker at the bottom than at the top. In both of these cases, the model would benefit visually from replacing the shields. Another case is when the original ship had open railings with canvas 'dodgers', but the model shows these as a solid moulding. The shields on the Tamiya *Indianapolis* are actually pretty good, and with a couple of exceptions, one could get a very reasonable result by just thinning the plastic slightly by scraping. However, I decided to replace most of the shields, in order to demonstrate the technique for doing so.

There are several different materials that can be used to make the shields; for example, 5thou or 10thou plastic card, or paper stiffened with thin CA glue. I used brass shim, 2thou thick, that I obtained

from a model railway shop. This is fairly easy to cut and fold, and has an advantage over plastic, which would seem the obvious choice, in that any fold or bend is retained. Plastic has a tendency to straighten out until it is firmly glued in place.

For instructions on how to cut, bend and curve metal strips, I refer you to the previous chapter.

53.

52.

I removed the moulded-on splinter shields using a sprue cutter, followed by a scalpel held horizontally, and finally sanding sticks. The brass strips are glued to the outside vertical edge of the plastic deck. This widens the final construction by a few thousandths of an inch, so I took a few strokes of a file along the edge of each part of deck where a splinter shield will be fitted. You can also see strips of brass shaped and ready for gluing. I hold the shields in exact position with pieces of Blu-Tack, or tiny strips of masking tape, and then run thin CA glue into the joint. Any gaps I can later fill with diluted PVA.

53.

As moulded, the shields on the forward deckhouse were inaccurate. The Bofors shield was set about 1mm too low, and the Oerlikon shield in front of it looked like the box hedge that I mentioned earlier. Both needed to come off. The larger Bofors shield was simply made in one part. After it had been glued to the deck-house, I fitted a piece of 5thou plasticard underneath it as a deck extension and trimmed off the excess. The smaller Oerlikon shield is a more complex shape and I made it in three parts. There is a quarter circle in the middle, and an open rectangle on each side to protect the ammunition lockers. If I had decided to make this small shield in one part, it would have entailed exact positioning of five folds and a curve. This would have been incredibly difficult. As it is, the appearance is a great improvement over the original moulding.

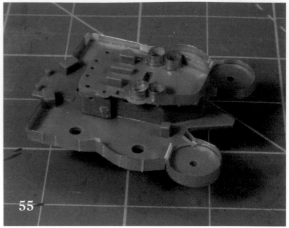

54.

The various bridge platforms. The signal bridge (top left) has four pieces of brass each side of varying heights. A curved piece of plastic represents a lookout station. There is an oblique gap for the tripod mast leg and two overlapping pieces of brass represent the searchlight position at the after end. Nothing is fixed to the aft edge because the signal flag boxes will be fitted much later. I have also added doors and vertical ladders. The navigating bridge (bottom left) is surrounded by a total of nine pieces of brass, including circular director tubs. There is a space on the aft side for an inclined ladder. A wind deflector surrounding the forward end is better seen on photos of the completed model.

56.

The only splinter shield that I did not replace was that around the stern gun tub. I thought that this would look quite satisfactory if the plastic were simply thinned down a bit by scraping with a scalpel. After this was done, I removed the director tubs and replaced with brass in the same way as all the others.

55.

Here we see the after gun deck that was shown in one of the earlier photos, with all of the splinter shields fitted and reinforcing braces added from stretched sprue. The director and searchlight platform has four identical circular tubs, as well as a shield carefully bent to fit smoothly around its aft sides. I used diluted PVA to fill gaps and fair all the parts into one another.

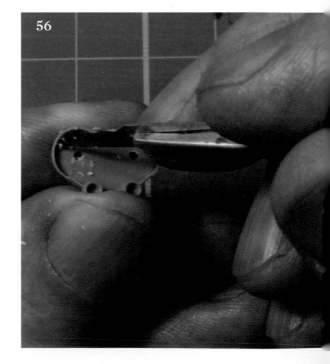

Masts

Because of the limitations of injection moulding, plastic kits tend to have masts that are too large in diameter and lack taper. They will usually benefit from being replaced with metal parts. Metal will stand up to the constant tension from lots of rigging better than plastic, which would tend to distort if it were thinned down to a realistic diameter. *Indianapolis* had tripods for both the fore and mainmasts. The foremast tripod supports the bridge and the kit part is best used for it. However, the mainmast is a complex construction that envelopes the after funnel and is not accurately represented in the kit, because it lacks any of the prominent cross bracing. In addition, the White Ensign photo-etch set has several useful parts that are set off by a good basic structure. But I did not use their parts for the tripod because the flat photo-etch is unconvincing for the tubular tripod legs.

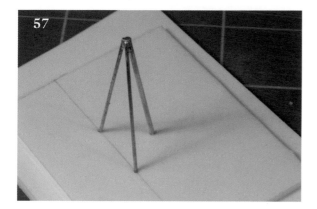

57.

Using the kit mast as a guide for measuring, I cut tripod legs from suitably sized brass rod, and made a jig by drilling holes in plastic card, again marking the positions from the kit part. The legs can be steadied in their holes with a bit of PVA glue, because this will make it easier to join the upper ends. I seriously recommend soldering. It is not difficult to solder a joint such as this, and it is far stronger than either epoxy or CA.

58.

I built up the cross bracing using stretched sprue and CA glue. This was a fiddly process and took quite a lot of trial and error. Using photos of the ship I managed to judge the spacing of the horizontal members. The kit part is of no use because it does not try to show them and the White Ensign photo-etch appears to have the wrong proportions. The diagonals are not strictly accurate because the two pieces of sprue cross over one another, but this flaw is not too noticeable in this scale.

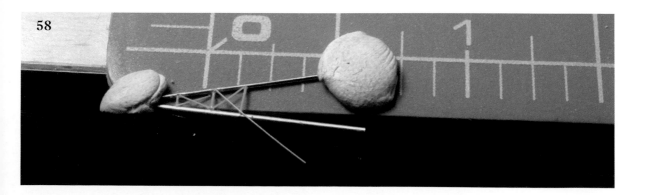

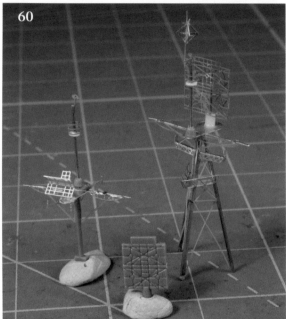

59.

The White Ensign set provides parts for most of the other mast fittings. This photo shows that I have fitted a triangular platform two thirds of the way up the tripod, and a larger platform at the top, with integral yards that have braces and footropes underneath. Another pair of yards made from folded brass goes just below the upper platform and these were quite difficult to get aligned and straight. On the larger platform, I put a small piece of plastic tube to mount the SK1 radar antenna, and a topmast from brass rod, with a tiny platform made from a plastic disc and a direction finder antenna from the photo-etch set.

61.

The funnels are moulded with the tops solid. I drilled out the tops and opened them out with scalpel and file. The brass funnel cages came from the White Ensign set, and were curved slightly before fitting. After taking this photo, and also after painting the funnels, I realised that I had not painted the interiors black, so the cages had to come off again. It was a good thing that I had used PVA glue. At the same time, I took the opportunity to drill two tiny holes on either side of the fore funnel, and threaded the funnel guys through. This was an example of how some forethought can save work.

60.

The completed mainmast (right) with the SK1 radar fitted. In front is the plastic kit part for this antenna. The improvement the photo-etch makes can be easily seen. To the left is the fore topmast assembly, which is made from parts provided in the photo-etch set, along with bits of brass rod and plastic. The plastic disc platforms on both masts have had circles of railing added.

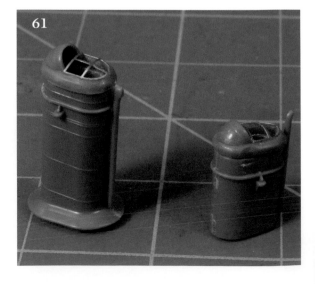

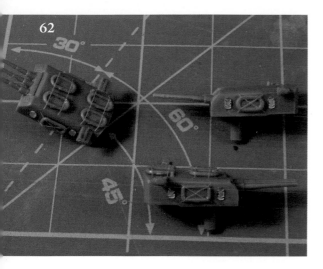

62

62.

The three guns for each turret are moulded together. I did not separate them because they elevated together in the same cradle on the original ship. I scraped the moulding seam from the sides of the barrels. Access doors came from the White Ensign set. I simulated retaining straps for the Carley floats by using stretched sprue. If I had felt really pernickerty, I could have used some more tiny pieces of stretched sprue as paddles, but I didn't go that far.

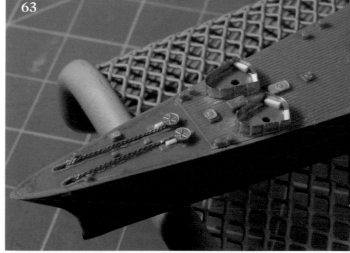

63

63.

Here is the foredeck, ready for priming and painting. I have fitted the anchor chains and added photo-etched brass tops to the capstans. Brass splinter shields for the Oerlikon guns with reinforcing ribs from stretched sprue are in place, along with ammunition lockers from 1mm square plastic strip. I am leaving the actual Oerlikon guns off until the model is nearly complete because they would get in the way of painting, and tangle the fibres used for the rigging. You can also see some steel hatch covers from another photo-etch fret.

64.

This is as far as construction of the hull can go before painting starts. Adding any more parts would have complicated the painting process. You can see that nothing here is obscured or masked by any overhanging part, and that makes it easy to get the paintbrush or airbrush on target. When this photo was taken, all of the other sub-assemblies seen in this chapter had also been completed ready for painting, as had most of the smaller parts that feature in Chapter 6.

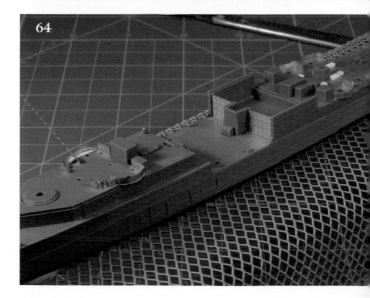

64

CHAPTER 5

⮞Basic Construction: Resin Models⮜

In contrast to the previous chapter, I now take you through the preparation and construction of the major components of a resin kit. You will see that there are probably more differences than there are similarities when compared with building plastic kits. Do not let the challenges put you off, though, because the rewards at the end might well be greater.

I have chosen a 1/700-scale model of HMAS *Sydney*, the Second World War cruiser that was sunk by the German raider *Kormoran*. This is a topical choice, because at the time of writing, her wreck has just been discovered. The kit is produced by NNT Modell, a small German company, and the owner of the firm, Norbert Thiel, was most helpful to me. It is a straightforward and middle-of-the road-kit, in terms not only of price, but also detail and complexity. Although the kit could be built up straight from the box into an attractive model of the ship, there are a few aspects that benefit from improvement, as I shall demonstrate.

The kit contains a small fret of photo-etched details, which is easy to use, because the metal is quite thick. I shall be adding more details from various frets by both White Ensign and Gold Medal. The 4in anti-aircraft guns will be replaced by Niko products, in the same way that I did for the Bofors guns on *Indianapolis*. Masts will be made from brass rod, tapered by hand and soldered where my skills permit.

My main references for the model will be the Profile Morskie publication on *Sydney*, which contains a full set of plans, and *British Cruisers of World War Two*, by Raven and Roberts.

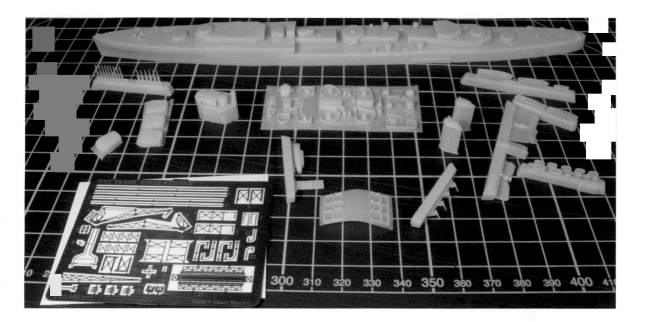

You will be struck by how few parts there are in the *Sydney* kit when compared to the *Indianapolis* kit. This is partly because *Sydney* has a much simpler shape, but also due to the resin casting process itself. Soft rubber moulds and hand crafting enable complex shapes to be cast as single pieces, which would have to be broken down into a number of components for injection moulding. The hull, with considerable detail and the bottom layer of the superstructure, is cast as a single lump of resin. This would take anything up to twenty separate parts in a plastic kit. It does not necessarily speed construction because more parts preparation will be needed.

The bridge is also cast as one piece, and in this case, I feel that it has resulted in oversimplification. As I got further into the construction, I found that the top of the bridge was inaccurate, anyway, but more of that later.

Smaller parts are cast either onto blocks of resin, from which they will need to be delicately cut or sawn, or onto a thin film of resin, which requires careful sanding.

Resin is more brittle than plastic, and some very fine parts are really beyond the technology. At the front can be seen a film with two frameworks on it. These are boat cradles, and they later disintegrated as I tried to remove them, necessitating scratch-built replacements. These parts would have been better if made out of photo-etch.

At this point, I should like to digress a bit and deal with a problem that is sometimes found with resin ship kits – the warped hull. It is possible with kits from any resin manufacturer to find that the hull is bent like a banana, either higher or lower at the ends than in the middle. I believe that this happens due to the heat produced while the resin cures. It can look like a disaster, but is fairly easy to fix. If heated to around the boiling point of water, resin becomes soft and pliable, and can take on a new shape as it cools. However, if heated beyond boiling point, it will become wobbly, like a jelly.

Find a cooking utensil such as a large flat-bottomed frying pan. It should accommodate the hull easily, without it having to lean against the side. With a very large hull, such as a 1/350 battleship, it might well be a struggle, and a polite letter to the manufacturer may be more appropriate!

Cover the hull with water, put the pan on the cooker and bring it slowly to the boil. It is a good idea to have tied a piece of string loosely around each end of the hull so that it can be easily lifted out of the water after it has been simmering for a few minutes.

Lift the hull out of the water, place it straightaway onto the kitchen worktop and remove the strings. The resin will be soft and easily bent. Using some folded tissue to protect fingers from the heat, press down on the hull to straighten it flat against the worktop. Keep pressing gently until the resin cools and hardens to its new shape. Try to avoid pressing on areas that are highly detailed because this will probably cause distortion. For the same reason I would suggest that the model is not clamped to a flat surface, as some people advocate.

Once the hull is back down to room temperature, the new shape will be permanently fixed, and it should not distort again.

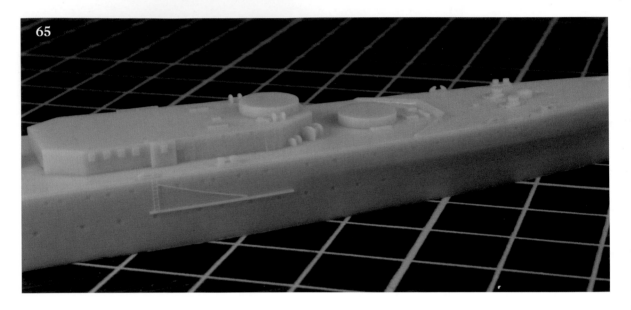

65.

This photo shows some of the detail moulded integrally on the hull part. Scuttles are in a perfectly straight line. If not, they would need to be filled, sanded down and then re-drilled, a total chore, and very difficult. Doors are visible on the superstructure sides – vertical ladders too, although not in this photo. Square windows with watertight covers look a touch on the thick side, but I chose not to replace these because I did not think I could improve them. There are crisp capstans, paper-thin breakwater and numerous cable reels that need just a touch of rounding of their lower curves. Although it cannot be seen, the deck has finely moulded planking and metal tread plate. A nice touch is a tiny rebate at the deck edge, which makes fitting the railings easier.

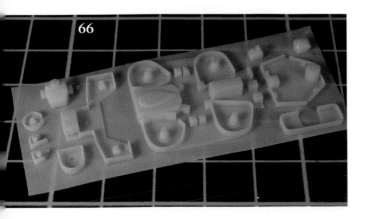

66.

Here we see parts for various platforms, as well as gun directors, moulded onto their resin film. The edges of the various parts are crisp and very sharp, and typical of this firm's products. Splinter shields are not quite as thin as some manufacturers manage to get them, but this does make them less prone to breakage. Unfortunately, as will be seen later, many do need to be removed because, in reality, they were actually railings. There is scope for improvement of detail, particularly on the gun deck and the main director.

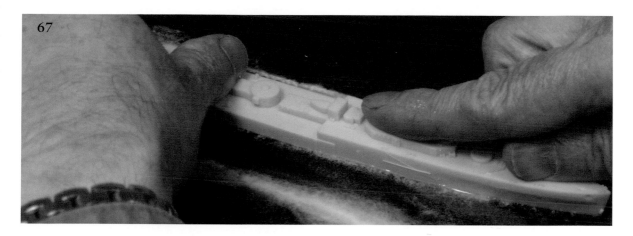

67.

At the waterline, the hull is cast with a slightly rough edge, which needs to be removed. Luckily there is not a large plug of resin requiring major surgery with a saw and grinding with a Dremel drill. The small amount of clean-up needed can easily be achieved by wet sanding.

I took a sheet of coarse wet and dry paper and stuck it to the work bench with tape, ensuring that there was nothing caught underneath to cause a lump. Then, with enough water to lubricate and wash away the dust, and even pressure over the whole length of the hull, I began sanding. I used a circular motion and checked frequently to ensure that I was sanding evenly. After just a couple of minutes, the hull had been ground down to the correct waterline and the rough edge had gone.

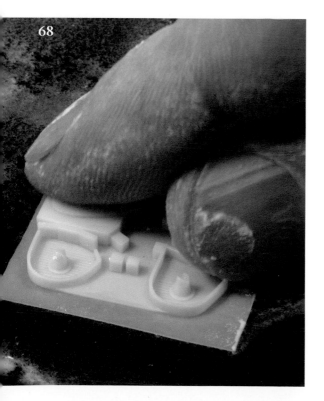

68.

Here I am using the same technique to remove the resin film from around the gun deck. It is very thin and I could have got away with simply trimming it away with a scalpel blade. That will only work if the film is of even thickness all the way round the part. In kits in which it is thick or uneven, it must be sanded away otherwise the superstructure will end up higher than it ought to be or have a noticeable slope imparted to it.

I try not to press too hard and I use a circular motion. I also turn the part through 90°, always in the same direction, after every dozen or so strokes. This will help ensure that the film is being sanded evenly all the way round, even if pressure is uneven. I still keep my eyes on progress to ensure that I am not taking too much off on one side. I also try to make sure that I am exerting some pressure on the centre of a large part to prevent me ending up with something that is thicker in the middle than at the edges. If I am doing it correctly, the film detaches itself on all sides at about the same time.

69.

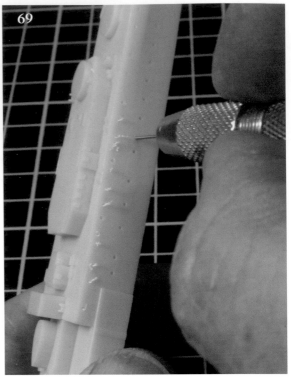

Drilling out the scuttles, in order to emphasise them. In real life, these would have been fairly small and it is easy to choose a drill that is too big. I use one that is about 0.6mm diameter, which equates to 42cm diameter in 1/700 scale. Using even pressure on my pin vice, I make the same number of turns in each scuttle, in order to end up with holes that are all the same depth. I do not make them too deep, and just enough to increase the amount of shadow in them.

If I wipe the swarf away from the holes with my finger, there is usually some left deep down inside. I therefore reverse the drill bit in the pin vice so that the shank end is sticking out, and push this firmly into each hole to ram the swarf out of sight, and ensure that the edges of the holes are clean and sharp. In this photo it can be seen that I am doing this on the lower row of scuttles, the upper row having visible swarf. Towards the top of the photo the scuttles are not yet drilled, for comparison.

70.

In this photo of the foredeck, taken much later in construction, it can be seen that I have once again used braided wire to represent the anchor chains. I felt that the ordinary three-strand plait that I used on *Indianapolis* looked a little flat, so this time I tried out a 'four strand square sinnet'. This is a more complicated plait but makes a convincingly three-dimensional chain. I used pieces of wire, each about 6in long, stripped from the core of hi-fi cable. This wire is of about 0.08mm of about 0.08mm diameter. For a battleship's chain, I would choose something a little thicker. I have draped a length of the finest chain that I have been able to find along the deck for comparison purposes. Even bearing in mind the fact that the chain is not painted, it is clear how much more convincing the braided wire is in its scale appearance.

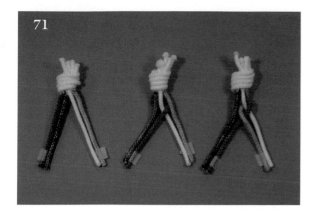

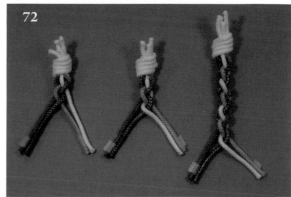

71.

72.

I should like to demonstrate how to braid a four-strand square sinnet. I am using nylon cord because I could not photograph wire well enough. I have also colour-coded the strands, although this is hardly practical with wire.

Left. Knot the four strands together at the end and secure to the worktop or in a vice. Separate them into two pairs, left and right. I suggest that you mark one of each pair, say the outer one, with a small piece of masking tape so that you know which strand is being worked on.

Middle. Take the upper left strand, pass it behind the others and bring it to the front between the two right strands. Take it back to the left and lay it below the other left strand.

Right. Take the upper right strand, pass it behind the others and bring it to the front between the two left strands. Take it back to the right and lay it below the other right strand. The original outer strands will now be the inner strands.

Left. Repeat the process with the new outer left strand, so that the marked strand once again becomes the outer strand.

Middle. In similar fashion, work the new outer right strand. After each strand has been worked, we are now back to the original position, with the marked strands on the outside. It can be seen how the strand that emerges from highest up the braid is always going to be that which is worked next, and in this case it is the outer left again.

Right. Now that a few more twists have been worked, you can get a better idea of the regular structure of the sinnet. When it is worked in wire, and it has been painted and dry-brushed, there will be something that looks quite realistic.

⟡ *The bridge* ⟡

The bridge was the major area of the kit that needed improvement. On the real ship this was a three-storey structure; the bottom level being completely closed, the middle level having an open gallery around the sides, and the upper compass platform being fully open to allow good observation. The kit has the bridge moulded as a single block, with the gallery represented by shallow rectangular depressions, and the compass platform having enclosed structures, which photos reveal to be incorrect, and might be a mis-interpretation of the plans. The sides also lack detail in the way of scuttles, doors and wind deflector. I chose to address all these issues by a major rebuild.

I am indebted to Norbert Thiel, of NNT Modell, who kindly sent me a second bridge part, so that I could demonstrate the process more fully in a short series of photographs. This kind of thoughtful and very personal service can only be got from small companies.

73.

To the left can be seen the bridge part as supplied; sharply moulded but lacking in detail. I had originally intended to use the top storey and only replace the middle gallery level where there are depressions representing the open areas. However, I changed my mind when I realised that the compass platform should have had no enclosed rooms. I suspect that having to scratch-build the top level was easier than the process that I originally had in mind. I have marked cutting lines around the part. To the right is the part with the middle level cut out. I ended up using only the 3.5mm-thick lower section, and the top deck was only used for taking measurements from.

74.

To the left are the parts from the previous photo seen from a different angle. To the right I have started building the correct shape of the middle level of the bridge by using polystyrene strip of 3mm thickness. When the bridge is finished, it will be possible to see straight through from one side to the other.

On the far right is the new compass platform. This was marked onto 15thou plastic card using the kit part as a pattern, which also gave the dimensions for the smaller raised areas.

73

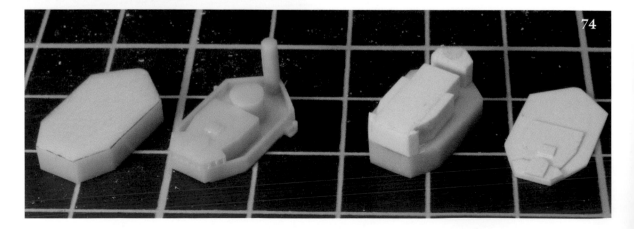
74

75.

To the left is a bridge with the compass platform attached. A piece of 5thou plastic card is cut, scored and bent to fit around the outside. I measured the gallery openings and cut them out very carefully. It took several attempts to get it exactly right. Adding a shell of plastic such as this will increase the dimensions of the bridge slightly. I tried to sand a small amount off the outside of the core but found that I could not do it accurately enough to avoid upsetting the angles. I therefore accepted the marginal increase in size.

To the right, one side of the shell is attached. I painted the gallery level bulkheads and deck first. I next glued the shell to the compass platform using liquid polystyrene cement, which gave me some 'wiggle time', and when I was satisfied with the positioning, used thin CA to attach it to the resin bottom storey. Some careful trimming of the forward edge was necessary to match the shape with the slight overhang of the compass platform.

76.

Here can be seen the completed bridge, all dressed up and ready for the ball. I covered the front of the bridge with 5thou plastic card. Scuttles were drilled, a handrail fixed around the bottom from stretched sprue and photo-etched doors glued onto the aft faces. The supports in the gallery openings are stretched sprue. The yellow parts, searchlight platforms, navigation lights and director tower were cut from the kit parts. The tall tower for the HACS director is plastic tube with a little platform and braces added from 10thou card, fine plastic rod and stretched sprue The wind deflector is based on a piece of 1/350 photo-etched ladder, with one of the verticals cut away. All in all, I am very pleased how this turned out.

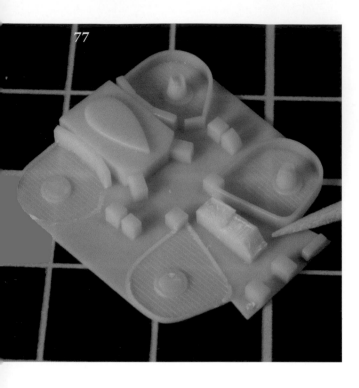

77.

The kit part for the deck for the 4in anti-aircraft guns has solid shields surrounding all four mountings. Photos show that this is incorrect. Those taken in peacetime and early in the Second World War show railings around the deck edge only, with no screens or canvas dodgers. There seem to have been no railings around the inboard sides of the gun positions – something that seems fairly logical – because they would not be performing much of a function. Later on, what look like canvas dodgers seem to have been fitted and painted to match the camouflage pattern.

It can be seen that I am removing all the solid shields. I will fix railings during the later stages of construction. I am also removing a featureless rectangular block of resin, as indicated by the cocktail stick. This is supposed to represent a framework enclosing spare wings for the Walrus aircraft. I think it is quite easy to make something more convincing and this is shown in Chapter 7.

78.

I have added some details to the gun deck. The correct number of ammunition lockers has been represented with plastic strip and photo-etched hatch covers, taken from the White Ensign *Southampton*-class set. The rectangular structures beside the funnel base are boiler room intakes. I represented the mesh that covered the openings with pieces of textured metal foil from a cigarette packet that I picked up in the street. On top of these, are glued photo-etched rectangles with diagonals from the same *Southampton*-class set. The metal foil was used elsewhere on the model, in front of the forward funnel, and on the sides of the catapult housing, where the same type of mesh seems to have been used.

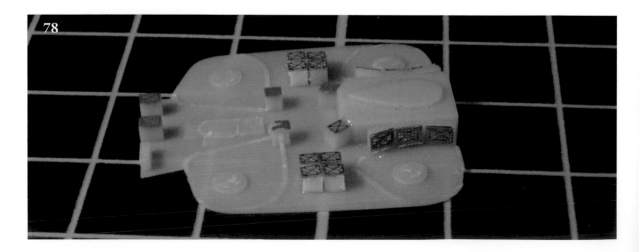

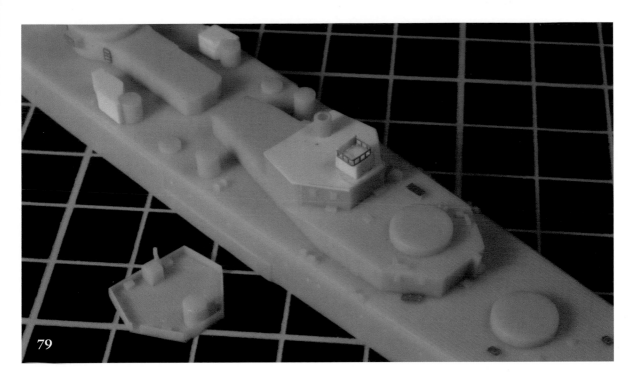

79.

The kit provides a five-sided deck for the upper level of the aft superstructure. This appears incorrect because it has engraved planking, solid splinter shields and a rectangular aerial trunk that should really be cylindrical and positioned off-centre. I replaced the whole part with a piece of 15thou plastic card to represent the steel deck. The little shelter was made of a couple of pieces of plastic strip with 1/350 scale photo-etched ladder for the windows. It will have the platform for the quad 0.5in mounting fixed on top. Open railings will go around the deck later. Further forward (top left of photo), I added a small deckhouse on each side of the ship, adjoining the mounting pillar for the 4in gun. These were not in the kit but obvious from photographs and plans.

80.

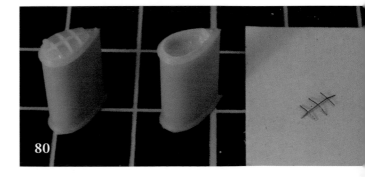

The funnels are moulded solid with a heavy representation of the cage across the top. I have trimmed off the cage and then opened up the funnel with a suitable cutter bit in my Dremel-type tool. These tools revolve at extremely high speeds and the cutters get very hot. They are suitable for using on resin, but if used for grinding polystyrene it will soon melt and clog the cutter. I keep looking for a similar tool that is capable of running at slower speeds

The photo-etched funnel cage came from Gold Medal's British Warship set. It has been trimmed to size and bent to an even curve. I have not drilled any holes for funnel guys, as photos show that there were none. This seems unusual for a British-built ship, but the photos are very clear.

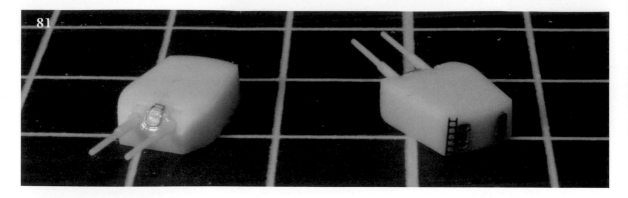

81.

A simple bit of extra detail was required on the turrets. Two fairly plain looking photo-etched doors and a length of ladder were needed on the rear face. There was also a somewhat triangular shaped door between the gun openings. I assume it protected the gun sights. For this, I took another photo-etched door, waffle pattern this time, and filed the long sides so that the upper end was narrower. It was also bent into a curve to fit the turret front. All of these parts I glued in place with epoxy.

I drilled small depressions into the gun openings to give a better grip for the glue to hold the guns in place. I ensured that they were not so deep as to make the barrels look shorter. If I wanted the guns to be elevated, they would have to be protruding from higher up in the openings, because the trunnions about which they pivot are further back within the turret. Epoxy was again used to give enough time to ensure that the guns were parallel in each turret and elevated equally.

82.

Sydney's masts were simple when compared to those for *Indianapolis*, being poles rather than tripods. The main mast had a topmast, so this required soldering of the brass. I tapered the brass rod without the aid of a lathe. I simply inserted it into a pin chuck and filed it, as described in Chapter 3. The yards were cut to the exact length and filed at both ends in turn. The pieces of masking tape mark the points where the masts will pass through the deck.

83.

This photo shows how I hold the mast and yard components together in alignment for soldering and gluing. The mainmast and topmast have been soldered already and the yards have been glued with slow setting epoxy. The whole arrangement is being put aside for 24 hours for it to become solid. I filed horizontal grooves across the masts at the attachment points for the yards. This gave an increased area of contact and allowed a stronger joint to be achieved with less glue.

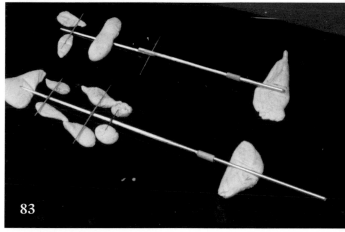

83

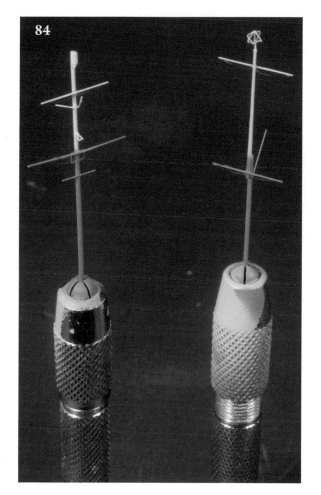

84.

These are the completed masts with crow's nest, aerials and other appendages added, as well as a coat of paint. It may not be possible to see it in this photo, but I have added a footrope under each yard from very fine wire, looping it around the attachment point on the mast and then securing to the ends of the yards with CA. I chose wire because it enabled me to adjust the shape of the droop beneath the yard.

This completes the major components for *Sydney*. Everything, including the smaller parts that will be built (see next chapter), will be painted before final assembly.

CHAPTER 6

～Adding Detail to Smaller Parts～

E ven though newly released kits have levels of detail that we only dreamed of just a few years ago, there is still room for improvement. In this chapter, I show how I use resin and photo-etched after-market parts and scratch-building, as well as some ingenuity and lateral thinking to improve the smaller details on both *Indianapolis* and *Sydney*. It should be obvious which ship I am talking about, but photos relating to *Indianapolis* are usually against a green background, while *Sydney* are against blue.

Let us first look at how a typical feature, the quad Bofors gun, is handled by different manufacturers, and the replacements that are available on the market.

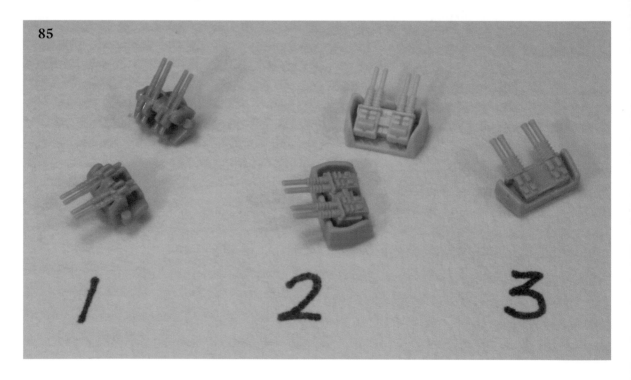

85.
_____

Here we see quad Bofors guns from various manufacturers. 1. Tamiya, from the *Indianapolis* kit. In fact, this is very good, and needs just railings and some sights. They do not really need to be replaced, and would look quite OK. 2. Skywave/Pit Road. Attempting too much detail on the barrels makes them too heavy. The mounting is a bit reminiscent of a concrete emplacement. 3. Dragon. The barrels look nothing like Bofors guns and really don't cut the mustard. But at least the mounting looks as though it would revolve.

86.

87.

These are some of the after-market quad Bofors that are available: 1. White Ensign, resin. These have been around for a few years but are still simple and effective, especially if dressed up with photo-etched railings and shield. 2. White Ensign, photo-etch. Extremely fiddly but exquisite. Unfortunately, they are overscale for 1/700. 3. Lion Roar. Not as fiddly as White Ensign, but the brass is a bit soft. Shields are all-in-one with the mounting, and that eases assembly. I would choose them if the model called for shields to be fitted. 4. Niko. An outstanding piece of resin moulding. The brass shields do not attach easily, but I consider these to be the best choice if shields are not needed. There is another firm called Voyager, whose products I recommend, but I could not find any in my boxes when I took the photo!

These are the 5in and Bofors anti-aircraft guns for *Indianapolis*, built up and ready for painting. The recast resin parts for the 5in guns needed a bit of trimming and the barrels had to be bent a little straighter. They are not perfect, but somewhat better than the plastic parts in the kit. For the quad Bofors, I used the Niko resin parts for the mounting. A cut with a razor saw was required to enable the footplate at the rear to fit easily. The gun barrels came from the Voyager Bofors set, because I thought that the Niko barrels did not look entirely even. I am glad that the model does not call for the shields to be fitted to the mounting, because they would have hidden much of the moulded detail on the front.

88.

Sydney's 4in anti-aircraft guns were replaced by Niko resin replacements. They consist of a barrel and a one-piece mounting. Like the Bofors guns, these are outstandingly detailed. There is also a baseplate that is not required and some photo-etched railings. I thought these looked a bit over-scale and used some more delicate bits from another fret.

89.

This is what I did to improve the gun directors for *Indianapolis*. I smartened up those for the 5in guns (left) by cutting off the circular radar dishes from the front faces. I replaced them by using some scraps of photo-etch for the mounting brackets and a circular piece taken from a cable reel for the dish itself. There is also a door and a couple of rungs of ladder on each side and a length of ladder on the rear.

For the main battery directors (right), I removed the radar brackets and the rangefinder arms. The radar aerial in its curved cover was cleaned up and kept for use. I glued a plastic disc to each end of the roof. 'A' shaped pieces of photo-etch were found to make the mounting brackets for the aerial, and I glued the whole assembly together with CA. Reinforcing members were replicated by gluing stretched sprue to the top of the mounting bracket, leading it to the edge of the plastic disc and thence to the bottom of the director. I bent some railing to go around the plastic disc on the right-hand end only. On each end of the director, I glued short pieces of plastic rod to make less stubby rangefinder arms.

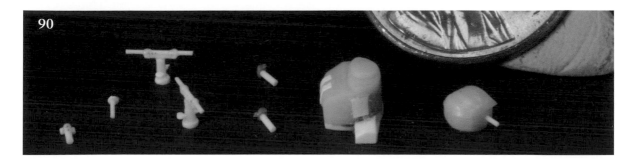

90.

90.

The compass platform on *Sydney*'s bridge is busy with detail. To the left is the binnacle, pelorus, rangefinders and lookout binocular mountings. I made these with scraps of plastic rod of various gauges, along with small discs of plastic produced with a punch, and the odd morsel of suitably shaped plastic. I suggested the shape of the casting on the mountings for the rangefinders by building up drops of PVA glue.

The main director needed some sprucing up, so I used a bit of plastic sheet as a base to deepen the structure. I removed the rangefinder arms and replaced these with plastic, which I then faired into the body of the director with filler. Sighting slot covers and access hatches are 5thou plastic card. The HACS director needed the bottom edge at the rear rounding off and rangefinder arms fitting.

91.

The parts for the *Indianapolis* catapult. I have just bent the main piece to shape on my photo-etch bending tool. The upper length of railing needs to be bent as well, in order to fit around the wider part of the footplate.

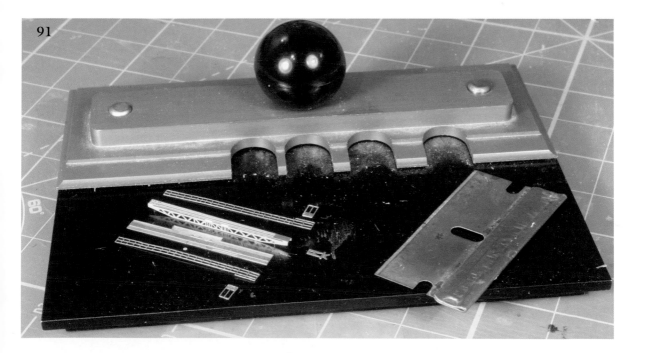

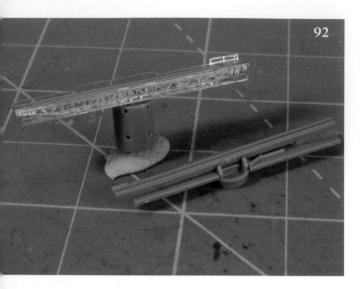

92

92.

The assembled catapult next to the original kit part. A photo such as this emphasises the vital role of photo-etching technology in the advancement of our hobby. I believe that this is truer for ship modelling than for other genres, due to the smaller scales in which we work. Using photo-etch is a vital skill to master.

93.

To the left is the photo-etched catapult that is included in the kit of *Sydney*. To the right is a catapult taken from the White Ensign's *Southampton*-class cruiser set. According to the plans included in the Profile Morskie book, I don't think that either is completely accurate for *Sydney*, but the White Ensign offering looks much more convincing and has greater levels of detail, including footplate and railings. I therefore chose to use this.

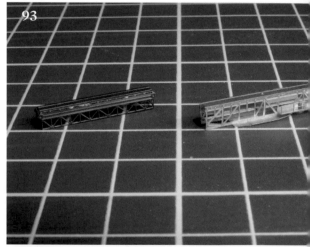

93

94.

The crane jib for *Indianapolis* from the White Ensign set. This is a delicate and fragile piece. I have gently coaxed it into a four-sided box structure. I shall be gluing it with CA and then filling the seams with diluted PVA. If I were not to do this, daylight would easily be seen through the open seams. The gaps will be obscured once the jib is painted.

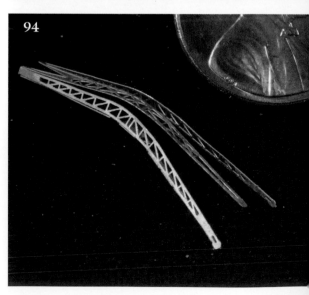

94

95.

The base for the crane was made from a couple of discs of plastic card. When they were glued solidly together with polystyrene cement, I drilled a hole to accommodate the vertical supporting column. I used Epoxy to attach the brass jib to the base, holding it in position with Blu-Tack while it set. I shall be adding wires between the jib and the pulleys at the top of the vertical. You may see that the final effect is a vast improvement on the kit part, which is clumsy in comparison, as well as being rather larger in size.

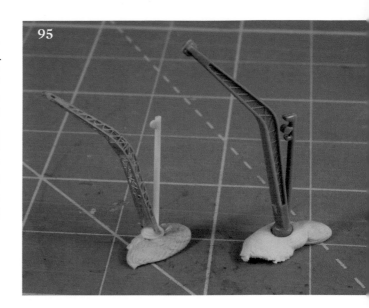

95

96.

This photo shows the crane for *Sydney*. At the left are the somewhat clumsy and basic photo-etched parts provided in the kit. In the middle are the equivalent parts from a Second World War British warship set from Gold Medal, and I believe these make up into something much more convincing, as seen at the right-hand side of the photo. As in the case of *Indianapolis*, I glued the jib with CA and then filled the seams with PVA. A piece of wire forms the hinge between the jib and base, although the final assembly is firmly glued and does not move. Inside the base is a resin part from the kit that represents the winch. The wires and pulleys are also photo-etched, and took some trimming and fiddling to get to fit properly.

96

97.

Most photo-etched Oerlikon guns have the cast pedestal represented by flat brass. The kit part was a better representation, so I cut off the shield from the pedestal, leaving a tiny lump of plastic to which to glue the photo-etched shield. In real life, the shield was positioned some way in front of the pedestal. Two barrels were added to each mounting, which were dual at this late stage in *Indianapolis'* career. I did not put any magazines on the guns, although I could have used slices of plastic rod if had felt extra pernickerty. In front of the Oerlikons are sighting devices for the lookouts, which will be placed at various positions on the ship. These are little more than a suggestion using plastic rod and copper wire.

98.

The kit parts for the quadruple Vickers guns on *Sydney* are just two-dimensional photo-etched bits. White Ensign includes these replacements on several of its sets for British ships. A total of seven parts build up into a beautiful replica that is not only fully three dimensional, but only about 5mm tall. I think that they are still slightly too big, but they are so delightful that I am prepared to overlook it.

99.

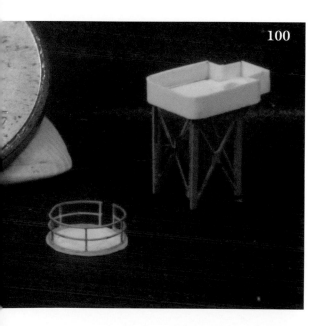

100.

99.

This is the searchlight platform that fits in front of *Sydney*'s forward funnel. I shaved off the top half of the splinter shields because photos show this to have railings around the top. These will be added later. The photo-etched legs were a bit simplified, so I added an extra pair of legs each side from fine plastic strip, placing them inboard of the photo-etched legs, and diagonal supporting braces. There are also vertical ladders on each side.

100.

These are the platforms on *Sydney*'s after superstructure. The smaller platform is for the quadruple Vickers gun. A suitable length of railing was rolled carefully into a perfect circle that was the right size for the platform. This was then glued to a piece of 10thou plastic card with CA glue. Excess plastic was trimmed back to the railings in order to give the shape of the platform. This sounds an awkward way of going about things, but I found it easier than trying to fit railings to the exact edge of a small circular disc. The larger searchlight platform was made from plastic card to a more accurate outline than the kit part and mounted on the photo-etched legs supplied in the kit. Transverse braces had to be added by taking a suitable piece of photo-etch from elsewhere. The *Southampton*-class fret is a good source for such bits and pieces.

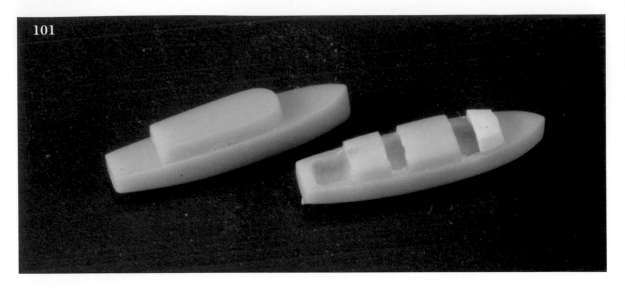

101.

102.

These are *Sydney*'s motor boats. They are supposed to represent an open launch with three canopies, which I suspect were open both fore and aft. I trimmed off the front of the cabin on the kit's boat and cut out a slot in the middle. The cabin roofs were given a curve from side to side. I then used my Dremel tool with a small ball-shaped cutter to open up the inside of the boat and also to hollow out inside the canopies – an effect that will later be enhanced by shading when painting is done. The front canopy was added from a bit of plastic strip, which I carefully trimmed to give the complex shape, and also hollowed out at the rear.

Sydney's Walrus amphibian consists of three neat resin castings, along with some photo-etch for the struts and propeller. I shall remove the moulded-on undercarriage, because I suppose that it would always have been retracted while on board ship. The two parts of the fuselage will be glued together and then everything painted by hand before final assembly.

Here we see the Walrus on the completed model. I glued photo-etched undercarriage parts under the lower wing in a retracted position. I fixed the interplane struts to the upper surface of the lower wing and this allowed the upper wing to be secured in place, taking care to ensure the alignment was correct. I found a small 'A' shaped off-cut of photo-etch for the diagonal struts under the engine. With care, it is possible to see that I have even added rigging wires to the aircraft, and for this I chose very fine black stretched sprue, because it has rigidity in tiny lengths such as these.

CHAPTER 7

∾*Bringing it All Together*∾

We are now at the stage where all of the major components are finished, although as separate parts, and the smaller bits are similarly ready for adding to the model. Now is the time to bring everything together and end up with a model that is looking nearly finished. Most of the parts are already painted, although that procedure is covered in Chapter 8 as a subject in its own right.

As we go along, there are many small details to be attended to, in whatever part of the model we are working.

103.

Here I have added two large parts of after superstructure to *Indianapolis*. The lower 5in gun deck was already in place, but here is a block of superstructure extending aft with the gallery above it. Further forward is the upper 5in gun deck with the midships searchlight and director platform in the middle of it. These are now firmly glued together. I have filled any noticeable seams by running PVA glue into them and touching up with paint. I have begun adding railings and inclined ladders where indicated by the plans. It is important to do this when there is good access. If left too late it will be much more difficult to get things positioned correctly. The metal parts have had a coat of primer sprayed on. Many people advocate spraying the final colour while the metal is still on the fret, but I find that bending metal makes the paint flake and it would be necessary to touch up anyway. Shiny spots can be seen on one of the ladders, and I shall have to attend to them in due course.

104.

A similar stage with the forward superstructure assembly. I have glued on the first two levels of the bridge. Note that I am using the tripod mast legs from the kit and not replaced them with brass. It is a lot simpler this way and keeps everything properly aligned. Again, a lot of ladders have been fitted, but this time some of them have needed little platforms as well. All of these will be painted in the not too distant future. Notice that I have put no splinter shields at the after edge of the signal bridge, where the two long ladders come from. This is because the signal halliards will be glued to the edge of the platform and then the flag boxes added afterwards, so the halliards appear to arise from in front of the boxes.

105.

This is a stage further on from the last photo. I have added the chart house level to the bridge. This needed some filling and you can see some smears of filler. This will soon be scraped away and evened out. I also added a rounded triangular platform underneath the director tub at the after corner of the navigation bridge. This is a mistake on my part, in that I should have noticed it from the photos much earlier. Well, at least I *did* notice it!

106

107

106.

This is the same stage from the other side. The fibres for the funnel guys can be seen. I drilled two very fine holes in each side of the funnel. A Caenis fibre (see Chapter 9) was fed through each hole from the outside and retrieved through the open top of the funnel. These were then knotted together and the loose ends trimmed. The guys can now be pulled tight without the need for gluing to the funnel.

107.

I first glued the aft funnel to the superstructure with polystyrene cement. Next, I glued the mast in place using epoxy. It took a fair bit of fiddling to get all the parts correctly aligned. I did not want to use CA to fix the mast because adjustment would not have been possible. Some green filler at the base of the funnel can be seen. This is because I had to remove it and shift it a smidgen towards the stern, and also to rake it a little more in order to get the mast to fit properly. In retrospect, it is evident that when I built the mast, I brought the two rear legs too close together at the top, so that I ended with insufficient space to accommodate the funnel easily. However, the general appearance is basically OK, and I am happy with it.

108.

This is the relatively simple method that I use to get railings perfectly positioned before glue is applied. Some people suggest attaching one end of a length of railing with CA and then working along, but any inaccuracy at the beginning will result in amplification of the mistake and distorted railings. I cut tiny strips of masking tape and stick them lightly to the hull. The railing can then be placed into exact position along the deck edge. Only after I have adjusted it and am happy that it is in contact with the deck all along its length, will I glue it. I use PVA glue diluted with a bit of water, so that it can be applied with a fine brush. This is strong enough to hold things and also has a gap filling quality. Provided you have chosen railings that have a continuous rail going along the bottom,

108

rather than individual stanchions, the glue will be drawn into the joint line by capillary action. This piece of railing has not been painted before fixing. This is to get it to show up well in the photo. I usually give at least one coat of primer.

109.

I do not use CA for fixing railings, apart from very small pieces. This is because changes in temperature can cause differential expansion between the metal and the plastic or resin. CA gives a stiff joint that has surprisingly poor shear strength, and the railings may well pop away from the hull in very cold or hot conditions. PVA gives a joint with more flexibility. If PVA is used and the

railings are cut into lengths of no more than 2 or 3 inches, there should not be a problem. In this photo, it can be seen that the funnel guys have been secured to the railings around the first level of superstructure and then trimmed off. I have also fixed a low railing around the forward end of the first level. This is just ordinary three-bar railing with two thirds cut off.

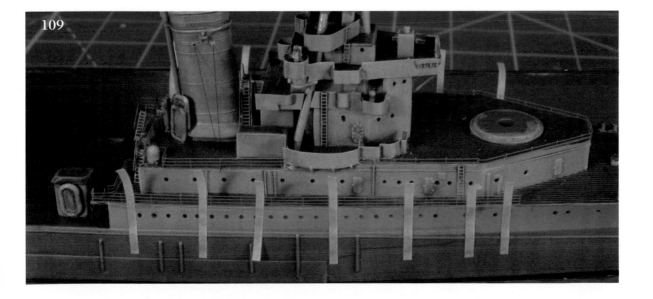

109

110

110.

This photo shows *Indianapolis* at the stage where nearly all of the construction has finished. I have still to do the surface of the sea and the rigging. Other little touches like the floatplane, crew figures and flags have still to go on, but even at this stage the model is developing a real sense of character.

111.

The foredeck of *Sydney* with railings in place. I have previously given these a coat of primer, but will later paint them to match the camouflage scheme. This may or may not be correct, but looks good. When applying the PVA glue, some slight smears may get onto the side of the hull on which long hours have been spent painting. This does not matter because the shiny spots will disappear when sprayed with a final coat of matt varnish. It is barely visible, but one might just be able to make out a junction between two lengths of railing, on the far side of the ship at the second stanchion aft of the breakwater.

111

112.

Sydney's bridge has been fitted to the ship and the various directors, rangefinders, etc., glued in place. I added a length of vertical ladder and some curved railing to the tower for the HACS director. I have still to put an access ladder onto the main director.

Lower down, the dark grey signal platform, with wings for the quad Vickers guns is now in place. I lowered the splinter shields and added a bit of railing on top, as well as taking all the shields from the aft part, where flag lockers will go. In front of the funnel, I put half open shutters on the inlets for the boiler room ventilator, and on top of this, a Carley float, lockers and the galley chimney pipe. I used brass wire for the whistle pipes and a photo-etch platform near the top of the funnel.

113.

I drilled a hole for the foremast, making sure that I got the correct angle for the fore and aft rake, and that it was also absolutely vertical in the athwartships direction.

Just behind the break of the fo'c'sle can be seen the beams for the larger boats. A photo-etched kit part supports the outboard ends. The kit supplied a resin part for the beams, but it was too fragile to be separated from the casting film. Instead, I made the beams from some fine strips cut from a spare fret of photo-etch. I used a strip of thin plastic card for the planking that gave the crew access to the boats. A cylinder glued at a slope on the side of the catapult can also be seen.

114.

After gluing the gun deck in place, I added inclined ladders, photo-etched supports under the 4in mountings and railings around all the parts of the superstructure. It is not very obvious in this photo because it is not yet painted, but I applied a film of PVA glue over the gaps in the railing round the gun deck to imitate a canvas dodger. I cut out four spare wings for a Walrus amphibian from plastic card, and after painting and adding decals, sandwiched them between photo-etch framing. This has been glued behind the funnel and looks much better than the featureless block that the kit depicted. In this photo can be seen how the platforms on the pentagonal deck are arranged, and the fitting of the mainmast.

115.

The completed bridge on *Indianapolis* shows that I have added the fire control platform to the top of the tripod. There are photo-etched supports under the after corners, but these are not visible here; neither is the ladder leading from the platform below. It is possible from this to get a good idea of the improved appearance of the gun directors, with added bits of photo-etch. The topmast, with all of its photo-etch, looks quite impressive, and much better than the plastic original. On the front of the navigation bridge is the wind deflector, made from a length of photo-etched ladder with one of the verticals cut off. I glued a fine strip of lead foil around the upper part to represent the outer plate of the deflector. Aft of this can be seen lookout devices in the rectangular sponsons, and below these, quad Bofors guns and an Oerlikon gun in their respective positions.

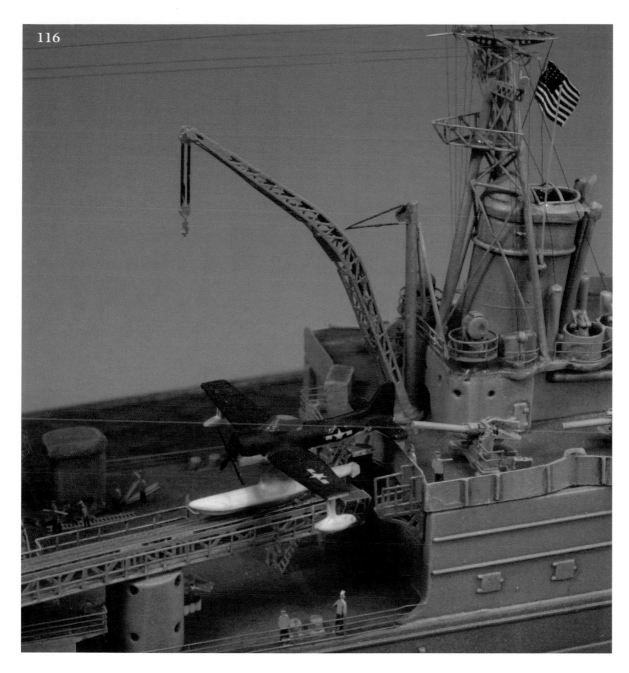

116.

I have added cables and hook to the crane and glued it in place using epoxy and constantly nudging it back to the vertical until it was set. After that I fixed a pair of supports from the top of the main column to the deckhouse, just inboard of the searchlight platforms. The Seahawk float plane on the catapult adds a bit of colour to an otherwise sober looking ship. I am never quite sure of the best way to paint the cockpit canopy when it is moulded in opaque plastic. I have chosen grey, but other people suggest silver or maybe green, to match the interior colour of the cockpit. 'You pays your money, and you takes your choice!'

117

118

119

117.

The aft superstructure is looking crowded, now that I have fitted the 5in and Bofors guns. At the base of the funnel can be seen aerial trunks from stubby lengths of plastic rod, the kit's Bofors directors in their circular tubs, more lookout devices in the after corners and a small circular searchlight platform on the forward corner. At the extreme left of the photo there can be seen floater net baskets attached to the sides of the superstructure, from the White Ensign photo-etch fret. I suppose that I should have put something into the baskets to represent the nets.

118.

I thought the area of deck in front of the aircraft hangar looked rather empty, so I put a bit of clutter about the place. Drums are stubs of plastic rod, cut exactly to the same length. The tarpaulin is a piece of cigarette paper, drenched with diluted PVA so that it can be moulded and then set solid. There are also lengths of plastic rod to represent some kind of pole and a ladder that is not visible here. The crew figures came from the Eduard set. These are sold pre-painted, although to my eye they appear a bit too brightly coloured. What do you think?

119.

The little tugboat is taken from one of Dragon's *Essex*-class carriers, which contain two as extras. The putative 'story' is that it has been towing *Indianapolis* away from the quay, and has just let go of the towing hawser, which is being hauled aboard by the men on the foredeck of the larger vessel. This does not make a very complex diorama, but it certainly adds a little extra interest and some more colour to the model.

120

120.

Back to *Sydney*, to look at the completed model. I took this photo at a deliberately low angle to show how it is now possible to look right through the bridge structure. 'Daylight' is visible at the gallery level, three quarters of the way from the front. There is also a good view of the semaphore platform fitted behind the mast. This was not included in the kit, but is apparent from the plans in the Morskie book. Just forward of the break of the fo'c'sle is the cutter on its chocks and with photo-etched davits.

121.

This photo is taken from a similar angle to an earlier photo, so it can be seen which things have been added. On the platforms at the after end of the deckhouse I have fixed the quad Vickers machine guns and a searchlight on a small circular platform. On the other side of the inclined ladder are the lockers for signal flags, two on the port side and one starboard. I have put boats and Carley floats in appropriate positions, and oars can be seen sitting in the cutter. Behind the funnel is the crane. As with *Indianapolis*, I used epoxy and supported it until it was solidly glued.

121

122.

Here we see how I have filled the gaps between the gun deck railings with PVA glue, which is then painted to match the rest of the camouflage. Depending on the type of paint used, it may take several coats to get solid and even coverage. If painting the railings before applying the PVA, and then only painting the outside of the film, there will be a pleasing contrast between railings and canvas on the inside.

123.

This photo gives a good impression of the uncluttered arrangement of this ship. Each 4in gun is mounted on a patch of planked deck. I expect this was to give a non-slip surface for the gun crew.

In the photographs in this chapter will be seen the paint finishes that I have applied. The next chapter considers how to go about this.

CHAPTER 8

∽Painting and Weathering∾

A s you have followed the processes of construction of these two models, you will have noticed that painting of parts and sub-assemblies has been going on all the time, but have noticed that I have not yet mentioned it. I shall now take you through the methods of painting that I use. But first, some very important questions need to be answered.

∽Style of painting∾

There are two basic styles of finish that can be aimed for in small-scale ship modelling; the pristine and clean style, and the weathered style. I will show my own techniques, and this means that I will deal with the weathered style. There are also many other approaches that can be taken to achieve the same sort of end result. I will not try to teach every possible method because I do not use them all or have not become proficient in them. I would not criticise another modeller for using a particular technique if it works well for him, because we are all different. What works for me is right for me and what works for someone else is right for him. That said, I do think it is important to choose the correct style of painting. The appropriate style to choose depends upon the type of model that is being built.

If building a full hull model, perhaps to be displayed on a polished base and supported on brass pedestals, it will look best in a neat and clean finish. This is the type of model that is seen in museums and such a finish best shows off the skills of its builder. You will aim for clean and precise painting, with smooth and even application onto surfaces. The colours will be exact matches for the available swatches. There will be no variation in colour, or washes and dry-brushing to emphasise detail, which will be required to stand and be judged on its own merit. But there will be no hiding place for mistakes. Any flaws in building will be shown up and magnified by this kind of paint job. Care and perfect preparation is of paramount importance. Scratches, gouges, uneven surfaces, etc., will all leap out at the observer, and probably when it is too late!

A model of this type is a celebration of the skills of its builder. It can be a thing of great beauty. But it is not a representation of real life, for we do not see real ships supported out of water on polished bases. Conversely, it would look somewhat ridiculous with faded paintwork and streaks of grime and rust. However well executed, it would tend to detract from the details of the model.

A waterline model mounted in a simulated sea base is a representation of a ship at a moment in time. This type of model really requires the weathered approach, because without it the model will tend to look flat and lifeless. Here you are attempting to simulate the visual effects of time, the environment and the light conditions in which the ship is situated. It is also shown in a relationship with its environment; the sea in which it is floating or moving, its crew members going about their duties, and perhaps other ships or the dockside if a diorama is being built. You will be trying to achieve this by getting subtle variation of tone and hue in your base colour, and emphasising detail by fine application of washes and dry brushing the highlights. As a result, the model seems to come to life.

This style of finish is much less even and precise than the pristine style, and to my mind is more 'artistic'. This is not to say that it is 'better' – it is simply different. To look at it another way, the pristine style is like a set of constructional blueprints, while the weathered style is more akin to an oil painting. Although not directly comparable or interchangeable, each is perfect for its intended purpose.

My models are nearly all waterline and I work in the weathered style almost exclusively. This is not to say that I do not appreciate the other style, it is just the choice that I have made, and which best expresses my personality. To me, a ship is more than just a steel mechanism. To the hundreds or thousands of men who served in her, the ship was their home, their community, their town. It is to honour these men, and latterly women, that I try to make my ship models come to life and have an individual personality. I know that this sounds hopelessly romantic, but it is just the way that I think about my hobby.

Choice of paint

Enamel or acrylic paint? This is another fundamental choice and will profoundly influence the way you carry out the techniques I shall be showing you.

Enamel paints, such as Humbrol, Revell, White Ensign Colourcoats and Xtracolour, in which the pigment is carried in an oil-based liquid, tend to be very easy to apply, both by brush and airbrush, probably because they take a long time to dry. This long drying time is also their major disadvantage. I have the impression nowadays that they have a less pigment-dense formulation than they used to, but this may be nostalgia for the days of my youth when I just scooped up the thick stuff from the bottom of the tin and painted away without a care! Different brands can be intermixed, and there is no difficulty about thinners, both white spirits and cellulose thinners work fine. I also think they are kinder to your brushes!

My weathering techniques involve several coats of highly diluted oil paints. The turpentine that is used as the dilutent tends to soften or lift the enamel if it is used for the base coat. This does not mean that enamels cannot be used, because a sprayed coat of acrylic varnish will protect the base paint before the subsequent coats are applied.

Acrylic paints are now more widely available than enamels. It is sometimes stated that acrylics are water based, but this is a misconception. In some brands, the acrylic pigment is carried in an aqueous carrier fluid, and others use an alcohol-based carrier or a formulation that contains both. It is important that the correct dilutent is used, otherwise a horrible porridgy mess will result.

Acrylics dry very quickly, so that they can be overpainted in a matter of minutes. As with enamels, this is both an advantage and a disadvantage. The speed with which it is possible to work needs to be weighed against the tendency for the paint to dry as it is applied, making it difficult to get a really smooth coat when hand brushing, and causing an airbrush to clog up and even for the paint to start drying before it hits the model. Some brands, such as Vallejo, are just wonderful to apply by hand.

One brand in particular, Tamiya, is notoriously difficult to hand brush, although it does go on very well with an airbrush. It is also extremely delicate if any alcohol-based product is applied over it. However, its range of colours does not contain many that will be of great interest to the naval modeller.

Most other brands give an extremely tough finish that will readily stand up to the punishment that my weathering processes will throw at them.

Airbrushes?

Aircraft and AFV modellers tend to use an airbrush extensively to obtain very smooth and even finishes to their models. They are, of course, wonderful tools for obtaining a flawless coverage of a surface. But when applying different colours on top of others and trying to get a sharp demarcation line, an airbrush requires the use of masking tape or similar materials. Ships are such complex structures, with numerous edges, fittings, decks, platforms and the like, that masking with tiny pieces of tape around every deckhouse, capstan and bollard, can be a tedious process. It can seem that using an airbrush is more trouble than it is worth when working in small scale.

My personal preference is to use an airbrush to apply major areas of the base colours, and paint smaller items, and often the decks as well, by hand. Even if I hand brush three coats of paint in order to get a solid coverage, it still seems quicker than having to bother with the hassle of masking.

Sometimes, however, the need to paint a subtle wooden deck as the first stage will cause me to grit my teeth and get on with masking so that I can then airbrush the vertical surfaces.

An airbrush will be ideal for the coats of gloss and matt varnish that form part of my method of weathering.

Nobody should get the idea that an airbrush is a vital piece of equipment and something that cannot be done without. My friend Jim Baumann, who is one of the finest small-scale ship modellers in the world, never uses one at all. All his painting is done by hand, and if he is putting on a coat of varnish, he will use a spray can.

∽ *Scale colour* ∽

The term 'scale colour' refers to the effect that distance has on the colour perception by the human eye. Another term for the same thing is 'atmospheric perspective', and I think this gives a clearer idea of what it is about.

When we view an object that is far away, the water vapour and other particulate matter in the air tends to disperse the light that is coming to our eyes so that the object appears lighter in tone and bluer in hue. This is one of the phenomena that enable the human eye and mind to judge distance, although less widely appreciated than size of image, parallax and stereoscopy.

124.

A view over the River Clyde, to Dumbarton and beyond. Notice how the grass in the foreground is greener than that behind the high flats on the other side of the river, and the trees are darker. Dumbarton generally appears lighter than the foreground, and the mountains get progressively paler and bluer the further in the distance they are. You know from experience what the colours are, but this optical effect enables you to get the impression of distance in a two-dimensional photographic image.

124

We experience atmospheric perspective every day of our lives without realising it. For example, in a new housing estate where everything is built with identical bricks and roof tiles, think carefully about what is being experienced through your eyes. If you compare a house that is close to you with one far away, it will be realised that the roof and walls of the distant house look lighter than those on the house that is close up. The materials are the same colour, but the brain experiences them differently. The same thing will happen when comparing the appearance of the leaves on the oak tree nearby to those on the tree several fields away.

This effect of scale colour has been used by painters for centuries. In a good landscape painting by Constable or any other painter through to the present day, the illusion of far distance is given by painting it lighter and bluer.

Modellers can use this same technique to deceive the eye into thinking that it is not 2ft away from a 12in-long object, but is in fact looking at something 700ft-long that is more than a quarter of a mile away. In other words, a real ship rather than a 1/700 model. It is simply a matter of adding a proportion of white paint to the basic colour. It has been suggested that the correct proportion of white can be arrived at by taking the scale denominator of the model, working out the square root, and using that number as the percentage of white to add.

For a 1/700 model $\quad \sqrt{700} = 26.4 \quad$ Add approximately 26% white.

For a 1/350 model $\quad \sqrt{350} = 18.7 \quad$ Add approximately 19% white.

The question of scale colour is controversial, with protagonists on both sides of the argument. Some recommend its use while others regard it as totally spurious and an excuse for not properly taking care with matching colours. My own view is that it can be of use in the type of weathered and lifelike style that I am describing. Dark colours, such as the Navy Blue Measure 21, can look particularly intense and strident when applied at full strength on a small-scale model, and will be more convincing if toned down a bit. However, a full hull, museum style model, probably ought to have full strength paint applied, but the real answer is that it is all in the eyes of the beholder.

❧ *Let's get painting* ❧

My system for weathered painting consists of a series of layers of paint, which by and large have the effect of changing and enhancing the appearance of the base colour.

The full series is:

1. Primer layer.
2. Base colours, including camouflage pattern, if appropriate, and decks.
3. Acrylic gloss varnish to protect the base colour.
4. Filters to give variation to the base colour.
5. Pin wash to emphasise details.
6. Dry brushing highlights to complement the pin wash.
7. Little bits and pieces.
8. Matt varnish.

Primer

A primer layer of totally matt paint is very important to an even finish. Paint will adhere much better if it has a surface with a bit of 'tooth' to grip to. Your model may well consist of several different materials – plastic of various colours, resin and metal, brass or steel. The paints to be used for the base coat will have different covering qualities if they are applied directly onto these materials. It might take many coats of paint to disguise the transition between plastic and brass, for example. A thick layer of paint is precisely what is not required, because fine detail will eventually be lost. A good primer coat gives a clean surface on which to work.

Spray cans of acrylic primer paint are widely available and not too expensive. I always tend to use automotive primer from Halfords (a UK store). This is available in white and grey. White is probably a better choice if the colour scheme is very light in tone. If it is dark, choose the grey, which is approximately equivalent to American neutral gray. Tamiya makes another good product, and this is a

125.

The stern of *Indianapolis* after a coat of Halford's grey primer. The brass parts, the propeller guard and the tubs for the Bofors directors have uniform covering. But notice how the primer has emphasised the flaws in construction. Glue marks around the points where the prop guard attaches and incomplete removal of the moulded-on boat boom are now very obvious and need to be rectified before any more paint is applied.

very light grey that does not easily show through the base colour.

First, prepare the model surface to accept the paint by washing it carefully to remove grease, mould release agent and fingerprints. Warm water with washing up liquid and a soft brush should suffice. Rinse thoroughly in warm water and allow everything to dry. I usually put the small parts into a kitchen strainer or sieve and run the hot tap through it all. Just make sure that some of the tiniest parts are not washed down the plughole! Bear in mind that if the model is hollow, water will get inside through any location holes. Shake most of the water out and dry everything overnight on a radiator or in the airing cupboard.

Have some way of avoiding touching the parts while painting them. I fix the hull with Blu-Tack to an upturned pen tray or desk tidy that I got from IKEA several years ago and the small parts to medical tongue depressors, again using Blu-Tack or double-sided tape.

The can of primer will give a fairly heavy spray. Begin the spray off the model and make single brisk passes without stopping. Do it from both sides, above, from bow and from stern. Hold the can about two feet from the model to avoid drenching it in paint. Even so, you will probably find that you have a fairly thick and wet layer of paint. This does not matter all that much, because the primer paint tends to have a relatively low proportion of pigment in it, and as the carrier liquid evaporates the paint film pulls up very tight to the surface.

The primer will dry in less than 10 minutes and if there are areas that need another swift pass with the spray can, these will be seen.

Now that the primer coat is applied and dry, do not be in too much of a hurry to get on to the next stage. Another effect of the primer coat is to show up any flaws that have been made in the model so far. Gaps that are insufficiently filled, uneven surfaces that need more trimming or sanding and hairs and bits of grit that have adhered to the model, will all stand out like a sore thumb. This is the last chance to sort them out before moving on to the interesting bits.

Wooden decks

The reason that I am starting off the sequence of painting processes with the potentially challenging subject of wooden decks is simple. If I am trying to represent a plain wooden deck, it is usually the first thing that I do. Masking is going to be necessary, and I find it easier to apply masking materials to a flat deck than to vertical structures. If I painted the deck after the hull and superstructure, my hand movements would feel inhibited.

The question of how to best paint decks to represent unpainted wood is often asked on the Internet websites that I frequent. Some people suggest replacing the plastic with thin plywood or veneer, even individual wooden planks on 1/350 models. The basis for this is the idea that real wood must surely be the best medium to imitate real wood. I contend that nothing could be further from the truth. Even the finest, silkiest wood has a visible grain that will look entirely out of proportion on a model of 1/350 or 1/700 scale. A skilful paint job will result in a far better representation.

What I do is this. I will usually paint a wooden deck as the first stage. Over a primer of white paint

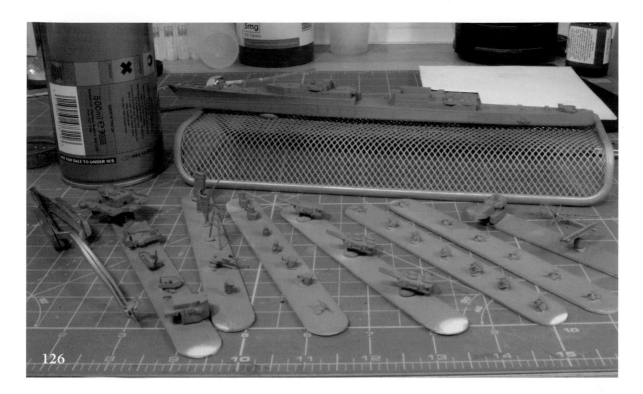

126.

All of the significant parts of *Indianapolis* primed at the same time. The small parts are held onto medical tongue depressors with Blu-Tack for ease of handling during the painting and weathering process. The less they are touched with the fingers the better. The hull is also attached to a temporary base for the same reason. To the left can be seen the can of primer. It gives a very robust and totally matt finish.

I lay a base coat of very light buff grey. I think it is important to use a subdued colour for the decks. I see many photos of models on which the decks are painted in a reddish or orangey brown that is very unconvincing. I go for a very light grey with a slight addition of dull brown. My personal preference is to use Lifecolor acrylic paint, which goes on well both by hand or airbrush. The mixture I use is based on UA 019 Sand. This is pale grey with a greeny-brown cast to it. To this I add about 25–30% of white and a touch of dull brown, such as dark earth. The colour I aim for is very pale and almost more grey than brown. I am not trying to get the warm and rich colour that I often see used, that is the shade of well-seasoned spruce. Even on a real ship, the decks would not be that colour, because wood fades with exposure to saltwater and sunlight, not to mention scrubbing, and is never going to be brown for very long. This base coat can be applied either with an air brush or by hand. Airbrush is a lot quicker because it will cover fully in one coat. It will take several brushed coats to conceal the primer.

Take some of the same mixture, diluted to a suitable degree for hand brushing, and add sufficient white to lighten it by a shade. A very fine pointed brush is then used to pick out individual planks. Choose them at random and paint a length of about 1cm for a 1/700 model or longer for a larger scale. Cover about 15% of the deck in this manner. Add some more white to the mixture and do the same thing again with this even lighter paint. The contrasts you are looking for should be very subtle and hardly noticeable. You may now take

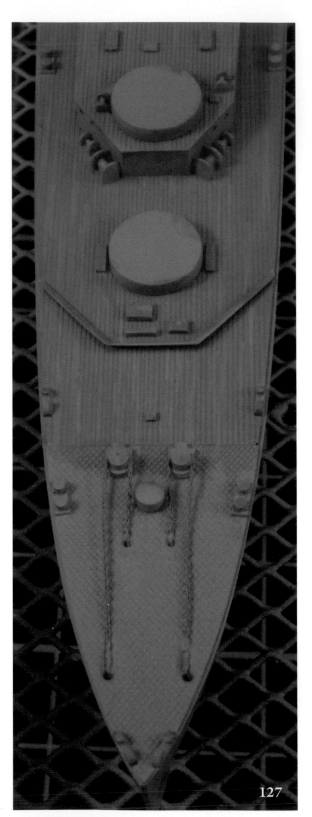

127

127.

The wooden decks of HMAS *Sydney*. The colour balance in the photography has made the deck appear more yellow or brown than it is in real life. The basic hue is actually half way to a pale grey, and not nearly as warm looking. Most of the surface is covered with the basic mixture, but you can see the variation introduced by the lighter and then the slightly darker paints picking out random planks. As the weathering process goes ahead, the variation will become even subtler.

some more of the original mixture and add a touch of brown to make a slightly darker and warmer shade. Pick out just a few planks with this colour, but not so many as with the lighter shades.

After applying filters to this subtly varied base coat, the irregularities that have been introduced will be hardly visible. However, something that is *hardly* visible is, in fact, still *just* visible, and that is the ideal effect that I suggest should be aimed for.

Base coats

Coats of paint will be applied to both the vertical surfaces and the decks, unless they have already been done as plain wood. It is generally good practice to do the lighter colours first and then the darker; however, if airbrushing the decks, then I suggest that those are done first, irrespective of the tone. As mentioned above, I think it is far easier to put all of the bits of masking tape onto the flat decks, rather than trying to put them on the vertical surfaces. On areas that are being hand painted, the order might be decided by how easy it is to get the brush into all the nooks and crannies with the minimum of mess to the bits already painted.

I am not going to try to give instructions on how to use an airbrush. I am not an expert in their use and there are plenty of books and articles available by people much better than me.

If hand brushing, then there are some suggestions that I will make. It is easier to get a smooth finish if using a flat brush and as large as is convenient for the area to be covered. Most paints will flow better if diluted a little, though not nearly as much as for airbrushing.

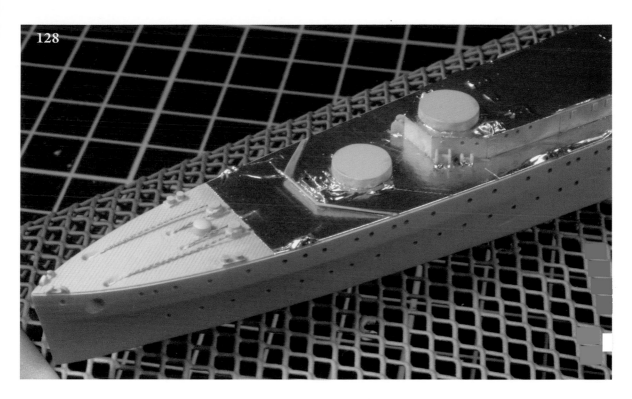

128.

The last thing I want to do is to spoil my handiwork by overspraying or smudging the deck with the other colours. Masking the deck is essential. I use mainly Tamiya masking tape, cut into pieces of various sizes and shapes. In this case, I tried something different – Bare-Metal Foil. This is a very thin and self adhesive metallic foil for natural metal aircraft finishes and chrome on car models. I found that it burnished down firmly onto the deck and could be pressed tightly into corners and cut easily with a sharp scalpel. It was a quicker process than trying to use lots of overlapping slivers of masking tape around the superstructure. I simply covered up most of the deck fittings and opted to paint them by hand later on. When the foil was lifted, it did not pull any of the deck paint away, although I did manage to scratch it with the tweezers, but that is purely my own fault!

Use vertical brushstrokes on vertical surfaces. On the decks paint a thin careful line at the junctions between deck and superstructure and then fill in the rest of the area, letting the brush strokes follow the line of the planking or using random strokes on metal decks. Try not to work the paint too much; it is not like painting a front door. Apply a stroke of paint and immediately do another stroke next to it, avoiding any gaps.

It is unlikely that a single coat will be sufficient. If, however, it appears that it is, it is probably being painted on too thick. I usually find that using three thin coats is about right. One coat must be allowed to fully dry before another is applied. With acrylics, an hour or so is enough, but enamels must be left at least overnight to cure. With each coat, brush marks will become less noticeable.

Do sufficient coats to get a solid and even finish with the first colour before moving on to the next. It will probably be found that there are some smudges on the areas that have already been painted and as a result be prepared to do some touching up when further along in the process.

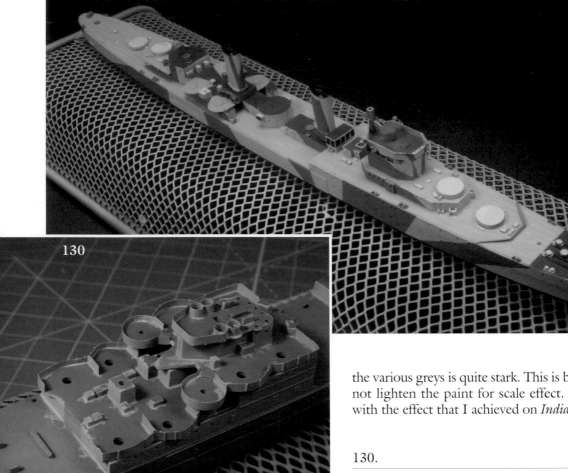

129

130

the various greys is quite stark. This is because I did not lighten the paint for scale effect. Compare it with the effect that I achieved on *Indianapolis*.

130.

I mostly used acrylics on *Indianapolis*, but I was not terribly happy with the quality of the brand I chose. The paints were all lightened for scale effect by adding 10% of white from the same range. This was less than the percentage suggested above, but I think these paints were actually too light to begin with. I used a dropper to ensure a constant ratio if I needed to mix another batch. I first airbrushed the decks with 20-B Deck Blue, and then the sides of the hull with 5-H Haze Gray. I did not mask the entire deck surface; wherever practical, I sprayed the Haze Gray at a very slight angle up from the horizontal and thereby missed overspraying onto the deck. I could not easily spray behind the splinter shields without hours of tedious masking, so did those by hand. As can be seen, I was quite happy to smudge onto the decks. There have been about three coats of Haze Gray applied behind the shields to cover properly.

129.

Here is *Sydney* with it base coats applied with the airbrush. The bridge, funnels and gun deck are just dry fitted, not glued. I used White Ensign Colourcoats paint. This is an enamel paint that comes in a vast range of colours carefully matched to original paint samples. Being enamels, these take longer to dry than acrylics and need 24 hours between coats. I first painted the dark grey decks in AP 507A and then masked them with more Bare-Metal Foil. The light grey was applied next using AP 507C. This was then masked using Tamiya masking tape and the mid tone done in AP 507B. Now that all of the masking has been removed, the result is striking and smart. The contrast between

131.

As mentioned above, I was not happy with the acrylic paint, which was sticky, had poor pigment density and brushed very poorly. Further painting of the deck was done with Colourcoats 20-B Deck Blue. This goes on well with a brush if thinned slightly with white spirit and it dried fully matt. Here I have applied several coats, first trying to paint precisely into the corners and then covering the rest of the deck with random brush strokes, attempting to hide the smudges and get a solid layer of colour in about three coats. There is still some unevenness in the coverage of the decks. This does not matter because the weathering process will deal with it all.

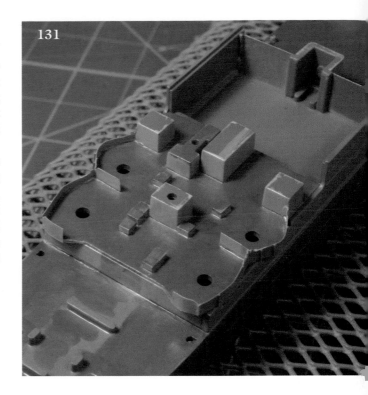

132.

Here is the hull and fore superstructure of *Indianapolis*. I masked the upper half of the hull with masking tape and sprayed the lower half with 5-N Navy Blue. Many think that camouflage Measure 22 is boring, but I regard it as rather smart looking. On the Haze Gray areas, there are some smudges that I have started to touch up and conceal. No-one is perfect.

133

133.

These are the bridge and after superstructure parts for *Indianapolis*. The main structures were airbrushed with Haze Gray and the decks and insides of the splinter shields painted by hand.

134.

Smaller parts for *Sydney*. The light grey gun turrets had the roofs painted first with AP 507B. This was because it would be simpler to mask the roof with Bare-Metal Foil, rather than the sides, which would have been necessary if the lighter grey had been applied first.

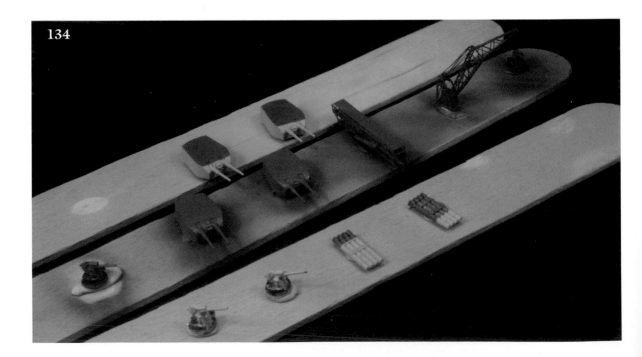

134

135.

This gives an indication of the sort of dilution of oil paint necessary for a filter. Only practice will really tell you precisely how much paint to use, but it should be considerably more diluted than would be needed for any kind of wash.

135

Gloss varnish

After the basecoat is finished, I strongly suggest that a coat of acrylic gloss varnish is sprayed over the whole of the model and the separate parts. The purpose of this is to protect the base coat from the subsequent layers, which will entail the use of turpentine. The acrylic varnish is vital if enamels are used for the base coat, but also useful even over acrylics, as the pin wash that will come later will flow much better over a gloss surface. I emphasise again that the varnish must be acrylic. Oil-based polyurethane will not do at all. By almost universal agreement, the best gloss varnish to use is Johnson's Klear, sold in the United States as 'Future'. In fact, this is not a varnish at all, but an acrylic floor polish. It is sufficiently thin to airbrush straight from the bottle, and gives an extremely hardwearing finish.

Filters

The first real process in my method of weathering is the application of a number of filter coats.

This is a technique that I have borrowed from our friends in the armour-modelling fraternity. The filter, as I interpret it, is a very thin and transparent layer of paint, intended to subtly change the appearance of the paint underneath it, breaking up the visual smoothness of the finish, and also tending to harmonise the various colours in a camouflage scheme.

Take some artist's oil paints. I would suggest black, white, a dark brown such as burnt umber, and a blue such as ultramarine or indigo, and also some artist's distilled turpentine for thinner and a soft flat brush. I suggest the use of artist's turpentine because it tends to dry much more

quickly than the white spirit that would be the usual thinner for oil-based paints in modelling.

Start with the black paint. Take a tiny blob of the paint and dilute with at least fifteen or twenty times as much turpentine. It should end up as slightly coloured turpentine, rather than thin paint.

Dip the flat brush in the mixture and then remove most of it with a clean, lint free cloth. The brush should only be damp, not loaded.

Working quickly, put random vertical strokes of this mixture onto the sides of the hull. The mixture should only dampen the surface with the thinnest film of colour, and not run at all. Do not try to get an even coverage, and in fact, only cover about half of the surface. Do the same on the vertical sides of the superstructure and small parts, and make random splotches over the decks. Apart from the damp marks while it is drying, the visual effect of a first coat of a filter should be just about imperceptible. If you notice something obvious, then the paint mixture is not dilute enough, so use much more turpentine.

By the time this is finished, the area where started should be dry. Repeat the process perhaps twice more with the black-tinted turpentine. At no time try to be even and do not cover the entire surface. Some areas have received three layers of the mixture, some have had two or one and some areas none at all. This is precisely what is wanted, and

136.

Filters applied to the hull of *Indianapolis* show, in particular, the paler tints, indicating the fading and chalking that occurred in the Pacific. Darker tones in the Haze Gray are extremely subtle, and this is what I have been aiming for. If I were doing this on an armour model in 1/35 scale, I should try to get a much more obvious effect. But that would be far too much on a 1/700-scale ship. It would make a cruiser look like a rusty tugboat.

when looking at the model after it has dried, it will be seen that there is a gradually developing subtle, random, and uneven appearance in the paint surface.

Now do the same thing using the white paint. I would not use as many layers as with the black, unless I am trying to represent US Navy Blue paint (5-N), which had a reputation for fading and chalking quickly in the harsh light of the Pacific.

A few layers of the brown paint are next. With this colour, I suggest more attention is paid to the hull rather than the superstructure, and in particular, to the bows of the ship, running down from the deck, where it would be expected to see more streaks of rust. The brown should also be applied on the decks, especially the metal decks.

The blue paint is the last to be used. I suggest that this is used on all of the vertical surfaces but not the decks.

These filters are to be applied not only to the hull, superstructure and other large parts but also to all the small parts.

When this is finished there will be a paint surface that looks a bit uneven. Some areas will be faintly darker than others, some lighter, some more brown, some more blue and every combination thereof. There should also be a suggestion of vertical streaking, but every effort should be made to avoid having any visible brush marks. Harsh contrasts between the different colours in a camouflage scheme will be toned down a little and made to appear more harmonious.

Let me explain my reasons for choosing these particular colours. Black is to give some basic tonal variation and to start breaking up the even finish of the base coat. It is also used to suggest a build up of grime. It is not there to emphasise shadows; that comes in the next stage. White is to represent some fading of the paint in response to weather, sunlight and the effects of sea water. American blue paints were particularly prone to this phenomenon, and I suggest slightly heavier application on these areas. Brown is to represent rust and other types of oily grime. We often see models on which rust streaks are painted using very bright reddish brown such as burnt sienna. I consider that this is too strident a colour for small scale. Real life rust stains show a variation of colour, and orangey brown is only a small part. From a distance, the different hues will blend into an overall duller appearance. Blue is used for a few reasons. It represents the effect of light reflected off the water onto the vertical surfaces of the ship. It makes everything look a bit brighter, more pleasing to the eye and brings some life to the model. Finally blue paint mixed with brown will produce a black or grey colour, and this a way of tying everything together visually.

It is also important to understand that these filters are not the same as a series of overall washes. When applying a wash, sufficient liquid paint is used for it to run into crevices and around raised details by capillary action. This is not happening here, where it is important only to moisten the surface with a very thin film of paint, which must stay where it is put and not run.

Pin wash

I have stopped using overall washes. I find them messy and difficult to control. There are always areas where some of the paint pools while trying to remove the excess, and this leaves ugly tide marks. The effect of an overall wash is to darken the finish too much for my taste, and this is an important consideration if colours have been lightened for scale effect. I have gone over to using a more precise method of application, known as a pin wash.

Mix a solution of artist's oil paint using mostly black with a touch of brown. This mixture should be a fair bit stronger than that used for the filters; perhaps ten times as much turpentine as paint. Take one of the smallest brushes and use it to place tiny drops of the mixture precisely on the surface of the model where shadow is to be emphasised, so that the liquid runs into grooves, recesses and around raised detail. With careful application, the paint

137.

The same stage has been reached on *Sydney*. Here we see among other colours a brownish discolouration on the bows, extending as far back as the breakwater. I added a bit more vertical streaking emanating from the hawse pipe and the various bollards and fairleads at the edge of the deck. Once again, the colour balance of the photograph has made the colours a bit brighter and warmer than they are in real life, emphasising the brown, whereas there is actually more variation in the greys.

137

138

138.

Black oil paint with a touch of brown and diluted for a pin wash with turpentine. It is a much stronger mix than for the filters, but still fairly dilute. Again, only practice will give the exact proportions. Here can be seen the type of brush used to apply a pin wash, and I put a little bit of the mixture around the lumps moulded on the palette so as to show the effect aimed for.

139.

Here I am applying a pin wash to the side of *Indianapolis'* hull. Here again can be seen the small brush that I am using. It is size 00 or 000. A larger brush would cause me to lose control. I am putting the paint just where I want it, in grooves and crevices and alongside raised detail. It should just flow along these areas but not spread out to cover the whole surface. If I put too much anywhere, I will take a clean brush, dampened with turpentine, and use it to lift off the excess before it has a chance to dry.

139

moves around only in the areas where it is wanted and does not run over the wider surfaces. This might happen if the drops are too big. Work slowly and patiently. It is easy to go over things later on with a bit more paint if the first attempt has been too tentative. It is much more difficult to remove excess, especially after it has dried a bit. It can be done with a brush dampened with clean turpentine, but there is always the risk of damaging the effect of the filters that time has been spent working on.

The main purpose of the pin wash is to emphasise the detail on the model by mimicking shadows. It is worthwhile making the pin washes darker in areas that are already in shadow. Another purpose is to represent heavier and more localised streaks of rust and grime than can be suggested by the filters. Add some vertical streaks on the hull, leading down from points from which water and rust might be expected to run, such as hawse pipes, breakwaters and bollards. also It will be noticed from photos of real ships that grimy streaks run down from scuttles (portholes) and other such openings in the hull, so it may be worth doing this if representing a very dirty vessel. For very rusty streaks, such as from the hawse pipes, use a brown pin wash rather than black.

Pin washes should always be applied over a gloss surface. If applied to matt paint, the granular surface will catch the pigments and cause staining, rather than allowing a free flow of the paint. This is another reason for using the coat of Johnson's Klear.

140.

Sydney's aft superstructure and hull. The pin wash makes the edge of the armour belt stand out, albeit with a small smudge that will need to be dealt with. Of particular note is the treatment of the 'waffle pattern' watertight doors. Here, I have tried to get the pin wash mostly in the upper left-hand corner of each recessed panel, to give the impression of shadows cast by light coming from one direction. The pin wash also emphasises the shape of the window shutters and the vertical ladder.

140

141.

142.

A pin wash has also been applied to the wooden deck of *Sydney*. I have placed a tiny amount of the paint mixture in some, but not all, of the grooves between the planks. The effect of this is to darken the deck somewhat and give it the grimy appearance that might be expected with operational use. The previous layers of filter have also lessened the contrast in the painted deck, as well as darkening it on their own account.

The dry brushing on *Indianapolis* helps emphasise the three-dimensional shape of the deckhouses and the corners of the superstructure. I have also managed to pick out the hinges and latches on the doors, the vertical ladder, the pipes on the superstructure and the thickness of the armour belt. Also note that there are no unsightly brush marks – a sure giveaway of rushed or heavy-handed work.

Dry brushing

By this stage, the various components and subassemblies of the model should be looking much more interesting than they were. The next stage will really make things come to life.

Take the artist's oil paints and make up a mixture that is noticeably lighter in tone than the base colour over which it is to be applied. Do not make it too bright. For US Navy Blue or Deck Blue mix a medium blue/grey. For a medium grey base coat mix a light grey, and for a light grey mix a very light grey or off white. Do not use any thinner in the mixture; the paint should be as it comes out of the tube.

Take a middle-sized brush; preferably a brush that is a bit too old and manky for painting, just as long as it clean and dry of any thinners. Take a little bit of the paint on the brush and then use a clean lint free cloth to remove all but a trace of the paint from it.

Now using a swift flicking motion, brush lightly over the surface of the model. It will be found that a minuscule amount of paint is deposited on high points of the surfaces, on edges and on raised details. As this is done, the model will start to absolutely sparkle. The fine detail will become much more obvious to the eye.

Dry brushing requires delicacy of touch. Stop every so often to see how much has been put on. If brushed too heavily, or if there is too much paint on the brush, or any thinners in it, this will result in brush marks, which will ruin the effect. These should be avoided at all costs. If the ship is finished in a camouflage scheme with lighter and darker tones, different shades of paint need to be used to dry brush the respective colours. A very light grey or off-white should not be used on top of a black or dark grey. Even worse is dry brushing a dark grey

---

143.

Similar effects are seen on *Sydney*. The dry brushing has combined well with the pin wash to emphasise the shapes of the doors and the window shutters. In addition, the bollards and fairlead stand out more than they did previously. The difference should not

be obviously visible to the eye, but the medium grey panels were dry brushed with a medium to light blue/grey, while a creamy colour was used on the light grey areas.

143

144.

Smaller parts also get the dry-brush treatment. Here on *Indianapolis'* turrets, the Carley floats are made to stand out, as are the doors on the sides. The guns are made to look more three dimensional.

over a lighter basecoat. For our purposes, the dry brushing should always be a shade or two lighter than the colour that it is going on top of.

Bits and pieces

All of the previous stages have been carried out before the model is completed. Now is the time to complete the assembly. While putting together the various sub-assemblies, it is necessary to add a large number of small extra parts – ladders, railings, platforms, aerials and all manner of other appendages. These will need to be painted either before or as they go on, and some effort made to blend them into the model as a whole by employing a touch of filter, pin wash or dry brush, although there is no need to go through the complete process, but just enough to stop the small parts standing out too much. Even on the smallest parts, a faint touch of dry brushing can lift detail and give an impression of reality.

Matt varnish

The protective coat of gloss varnish that I advocate, combined with the turpentine from the filters and pin wash, will leave the model with a somewhat uneven gloss finish. Although this is not a problem during the assembly of the model, it is not appropriate as the final finish, which really needs to be totally matt.

After everything else has been done to the model, all details and small parts, rigging, flags, mounting on the base, etc., a couple of thin layers of dilute matt varnish should be sprayed over the whole thing, preferably with the use of an airbrush. If an airbrush is not available, it is possible to get matt varnishes in a spray can, although I have to confess that I have not found one that is really satisfactory. They tend to spray a very thick coat, and do not dry with a particularly matt finish. It is only in putting on the various coats of varnish that I really think that an airbrush is indispensable to my method of painting.

The finest matt varnish that I have found is obtainable from the art shop. It is Cryla Soluble Matt Varnish. This is an acrylic-based varnish, but despite that it is thinned with white spirit. It is quite thick in the bottle, but if it is diluted enough, it will spray beautifully through the airbrush and dries immediately to a totally flat finish.

Ensure that all oil-based washes and dry brushing have had enough time to fully cure before spraying with this varnish. The underlying layers should then not be disturbed by it. Try to avoid a heavy coat of matt varnish. A heavy coat will tend to accumulate in crevices and dry leaving a white residue of the fine mica particles that give it the matt finish.

This final matt coat will not only dull down the gloss finish, but also will disguise any shiny areas due to glue spots, such as those from fixing railings to the deck edges.

∽*Difficult colours*∽

Two colours present particular difficulties to modellers who wish to use weathering techniques. If black paint is used at full strength, then it is not possible to apply a wash to emphasise shadows, because there is not going to be anything darker. Similarly, pure white cannot be highlighted.

The usual answer is not to use full strength black or white paint. Bear in mind what I have said about the principle of lightening paints for scale effect. At a distance black will appear as a very dark grey. This is what should be used to represent black, perhaps with a touch of brown. The addition of brown may be useful in a Victorian colour scheme of black, white and buff, because it will help harmonise the various colours pleasantly. It is now possible to use pure black, still diluted, of course, as a pin wash. The addition of a bit of blue to the wash mixture will give the impression of an even deeper black, and is a useful trick to try. Now proceed to dry brush with a medium to dark grey.

In the same way, it is recommended not to use pure white as a base coat, but choose to use very light grey, or creamy off-white. Brilliant white, as we know it nowadays, is a fairly recent development, and the white used as a naval paint in the Second World War had a creamy appearance in comparison. Using off-white as the base colour is therefore more accurate. It is now possible to use a grey or brownish grey as a pin wash and then dry brush with pure white oil paint.

The photo below, a work in progress, shows how the filters, described earlier, can be used to modulate the starkness of a white finish.

This completes the process of painting a weathered model according to the methods that I have developed over the past few years. Other modellers will use different methods, and I do not pretend that mine are naturally superior in every, or even any way, to those used by my colleagues, some of whom are much better than I am. I have simply presented my own ways of approaching the subject, and invite you to use them as you see fit, and to refine them as your own skills develop.

CHAPTER 9

~Rigging~

Rigging a ship with a reasonable attempt at scale thickness and complexity is the part of ship modelling that I regard as my particular speciality. That is not to say that I always enjoy it; there are times when it gets infuriating and frustrating, and the model almost gets thrown to the floor. But, done well, the end result is enormously satisfying, and the model leaps at you shouting, 'I am the real thing!'

I see many otherwise excellent models that are spoiled by over-scale rigging. The first things noticed are the thick black lines, and these detract from the rest of the handiwork. Using the methods I describe here, this is no longer necessary.

But, first, let us consider the question of whether we should be rigging 1/700 models at all. In various web-based forums, I have read opinions along the lines of, 'Rigging is unnecessary. You can hardly see it, so why go to the bother of putting it on?' I would answer this by saying that if something is *hardly* visible, then it is, in fact, still just visible. We should therefore make an attempt at representing it. If we manage to get a scale appearance, then on first glance, from a distance or perhaps in poor light, we just get the effect that *something* is there, and this draws our attention in towards the model and we can see the full complexity, not just of the rigging but of all the detail work that has been done.

The rigging on a real ship is, surprisingly, visible, provided it is viewed from a suitable distance, comparable to the distance that you would look at a model.

Take a 1/700 model and start to examine it closely, not simply in passing, and it will be found that the distance from your eyes to the model is about the same as your comfortable reading distance (18 inches to 2 feet away), depending on the individual's eyesight. Multiply this by 700 and it will be equivalent to looking at a full size ship from a distance of between 1,050 and 1,400 feet.

This might sound like a long way, given that a quarter of a mile is 1,320ft, but consider the sizes of real ships that you might have the opportunity to

see. HMS *Belfast*, in London, is 613ft long, and so by my calculations you should be looking at her from a distance equivalent to twice her length. This should give an image on the retina of your eye the same size as a 1/700 model from an ideal distance for close inspection. In the United States, an *Iowa*-class battleship is 887ft long and an *Essex*-class carrier 820ft. These ships should be viewed from distances one and a half times their lengths. At these sorts of distances, rigging will be easily visible. When we look at our models, it is not the same as looking at a real ship way out at sea.

If you do not have the opportunity to look at real ships, you can play a similar game by looking at electricity pylons or telegraph poles and realizing how far into the distance you can be aware of the wires.

I hope I have convinced you that it is appropriate to rig a model, but how thick should rigging wires be? Let's do the maths.

Consulting a book containing reproductions of Admiralty draughts, the mast stays on a *Leander*-class cruiser were specified as being made of 3.5in wire rope. This will refer to the circumference, not the diameter.

3.5in × 25.4 = 88.9mm circumference

88.9mm ÷ 3.142 = 28.29mm diameter for the full size ship (π = 3.142 approx.)

28.29mm ÷ 700 = 0.04mm diameter for our model. This is a touch less than one twentieth of a millimetre.

To make a comparison with a material that most of

us have very close to us, the average thickness of a human hair is 0.09mm. This gives us a basic target to aim at. We are looking for material that is finer than hair with which to make the heavier parts of the rigging. Other wires will be of different gauges in proportion. Aerials and yard lifts will be a bit thinner than the mast stays, signal halliards will be thinner still. Mast stays for a battleship would be a bit thicker. On a pre-dreadnought battleship model, the shrouds for the lower masts will be much thicker.

Choice of material

Let's look at some of the types of thread or fibre that can be used in model ships, and then concentrate on those that I use.

First, I mention sewing thread, but only to dismiss it as a thoroughly unsuitable material. It is far too thick and heavy, being about 6in in diameter in 1/700 scale, and also has fuzziness from the fibres that make it up. Even for rigging a sailing ship in much larger scale, I would recommend something different. For our purposes, do not touch it.

Stretched sprue is probably the most popular rigging material, but it is subject to an unfortunate trade-off between thinness and strength. It is possible to stretch sprue to a diameter suitable for true-scale rigging, but it becomes so fragile that it will break if one looks at it without smiling. Colour is also an issue. Most sprue nowadays comes in a light grey plastic, and we should really be aiming to use black or dark grey materials to imitate wire ropes. A very light colour actually makes the rigging more noticeable, although a brown or tan colour might be appropriate for signal halliards. Jim Baumann uses stretched sprue almost exclusively for his models, and his work is exquisite, but I am sure I could not emulate him. If you manage to do it, then I take my hat off to you.

145.

On the left, ordinary cotton. Even in this photo, I think I can see the fuzziness. On the right, Caenis. Quite honestly, there is just no comparison between the two. Give the cotton back to your wife!

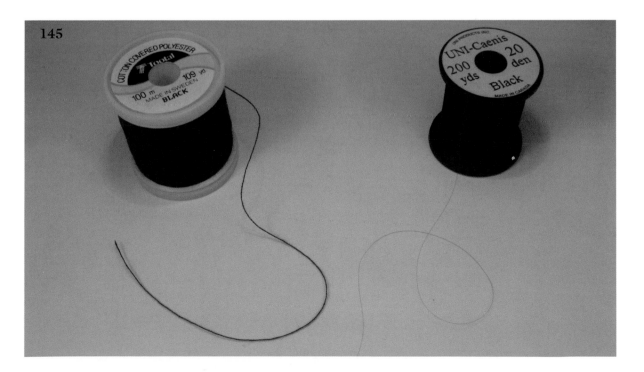

145

146

Fine nylon fishing line is used by many modellers, especially in the United States, where finer gauges seem to be more easily available than in Europe, but I still consider it to be too thick for 1/700 work, although it is suitable for certain elements of the rigging in larger scales.

Nevertheless, the fishing shop is the source of a material that has become one of my favourites. I cannot praise Caenis too highly. Produced by the Canadian company Uni-Thread, it is a black nylon monofilament intended for tying flies on tiny hooks. It is 20-denier gauge, and I estimate that to be approximately 0.05mm diameter. This is almost exactly what we are looking for. It comes on a reel, so is easy to handle, and is surprisingly strong. It is also inexpensive. Caenis is my current choice for shrouds and mast stays.

Nylon cords are braided from large numbers of fine fibres. If you choose a suitable cord, it is surprisingly easy to pull out a hank of fibres from the body of the cord. It is a matter of ensuring that the cord has an ordinary over and under weave and is not too tight. The fibres in the hank will not be twisted together, and a single fibre can be drawn out from it. This is another raw material for the rigging. Useful sources of cord are hardware stores,

146.

First, extract a hank of fibres from the braided cord. Once it has been winkled out from the cord, it is usually surprisingly easy to pull it out. In each hank (or strand may be the more technical term) there will be many hundreds of individual fibres, and they will not be twisted together. With good light a single fibre can be drawn out with no difficulty at all. Even though some of these fibres are so thin that they are nearly invisible except in good light, they still have an appreciable strength. Although the rigging will not stand heavy treatment, it will be much more robust than stretched sprue.

where it is sold by the metre off the reel, or the handles of department store carrier bags. Different cords will yield fibres of varying diameters, so that visual interest can be added to the model. An advantage of the carrier bag cord is that it will usually be dyed black, whereas the hardware store cord will need to be stained with a magic marker before use. Another, even bigger, advantage, is the fact that you get 'Brownie points' for your hobby, by encouraging your wife to go clothes shopping. Just as long as she lets you have the bags!

Although I am enthusiastic about the use of nylon fibres, I admit that they are not perfect. Coming as they do from a braided cord, they all have a kink and curl fixed in them and because of this they need to be attached to the masts and yards under slight tension. They cannot be used to represent lines that are drooping or hanging loose. These will be better simulated by stretched sprue or my other favoured material – copper wire.

It is possible to get copper wire from specialist suppliers in a wide range of sizes down to 0.032mm, thinner than Caenis and one-third the diameter of human hair. Alternatively, rather thicker

147.

Various copper wires. The left-hand reel is 0.032mm diameter, and all but invisible here. The others are 0.1mm and 0.125mm. In front is the core of high quality hi-fi speaker cable. This yields miles of wire, of about 0.08mm diameter.

wire of about 0.08mm diameter can be obtained by stripping out the core of high quality hi-fi speaker cable, or unbraiding co-axial television aerial cable.

❦ *Glues* ❦

My favourite adhesive for rigging ships is something you have probably never thought of using, and maybe never seen for years. Stationer's gum is what they used to give us at school (in my day, at least) for sticking paper. It is the amber-coloured stuff in the bottle that had a squidgy rubber cap with a slit cut in it. In the United States, it is known as mucilage. It has several advantages that make it the ideal glue for small scale rigging.

It is entirely strong enough to hold fibres in place. It can be diluted with a drop of water so that it can be applied precisely with a fine brush. It dries in a couple of minutes without leaving a significant lumpy residue. It is not temperamental in the same way as cyanoacrylate, which adamantly refuses to grip if there is any movement between the objects in question. Last, but not least, it is water soluble, so it is easy to repair mistakes.

147

Gum used to be easy to find on the shelves of stationer's and art shops, but has all but disappeared because of the introduction of the more popular glue sticks. But it is available on special order, although you may need to buy a litre bottle of the stuff. An alternative is gum arabic, which will be found on the art materials shelves. This is essentially the same thing, although more refined and perhaps more diluted. But I do not think much money will be saved by purchasing it.

In addition to gum, I use small amounts of thin CA glue when rigging. This is useful for anchoring a fibre into a hole in the deck or a similar situation, or where I wish to reinforce a critical point that might be subject to constant tension. I do not use it as my standard adhesive.

PVA glue is used to make little 'blobs' on the rigging, to simulate the insulators or connecting blocks that seem to be a characteristic feature in the rigging of British ships of the first half of the 20th century.

Other requirements

Tools are simple. You will need a couple of pairs of fine tweezers, straight and angled, with a positive grip at the extreme tip. Get some very fine scissors, such as might be found in the fly-tying section of the angling store, or surgeon's iris scissors, and a fine paintbrush for the gum and an applicator for CA glue. Some Blu-Tack is needed for holding the ends of the fibre under tension while the glue is drying.

Work in an environment where there is plenty of light, preferably coming from behind rather than in front, so try and have your back to the window. Work on a sheet of white paper to make the fibres more visible. Ensure that there are no draughts to blow them about the place.

Let's get rigging!

I am not demonstrating my rigging methods on one of the kits that I built for this book, because the fibres would not show up well photographically against the fully painted ship and the sea base. So I have taken another, simple kit, assembled the main parts and painted it with a plain coat of light grey primer. I have attached a few pieces of photo-etched railing and painted these black to contrast with the rest of the ship. A sheet of plastic card represents the base. As a result of this, the fibres will show up much more clearly.

148

I am simply demonstrating the techniques and I am not trying to portray the exact rigging of a British E-class destroyer. What I am doing is inaccurate in a historical sense, and I know it is inaccurate. But as soon as the final photograph is taken, I will remove all of the rigging and put the model away to be completed to my satisfaction over the coming months!

149

148.

First, some standing rigging. On a 20th-century warship, this consists of such things as the mast stays and shrouds, topmast stays and yard lifts. I am using Caenis for these, because it is the appropriate diameter. It is strong and very easy to handle. This piece is going to represent the shroud and backstay on the starboard side. I have tied an ordinary overhand knot or half hitch in the fibre and placed it over the masthead. I am just about to pull it tight at the appropriate position on the mast, just underneath the lower yard. I will then paint a small dab of gum onto the knot to secure it and give it a minute or two to dry.

149.

I have threaded the Caenis between the railings at suitable points, ensuring that it passes underneath the lowest of the three horizontal rails. The Caenis is held tight by pressing it into a lump of Blu-Tack under just enough tension to pull the kinks or bends out of it. It can be seen that I am applying a drop of gum to the point where the fibre is in contact with the railing.

150

150.

I have done exactly the same with more Caenis fibre to represent the rest of the stays, upper stays and the dressing line, running from bow to stern via the masthead. I am about to trim the excess fibre. These are the spring-loaded scissors that I bought from the fishing shop; the important factor is not that their points are sharp, but more that they have blades that are thin. This makes it possible to make the cut extremely close to the point of attachment.

151

151.

The standing rigging is completed. It will hold up perfectly well, despite the gum being intended only for sticking paper. For the sake of clarity, these lines will be removed from this model so that I can demonstrate the other stages without causing visual confusion. Obviously, I would not do that on an actual project.

152.

For signal halliards I use the very finest fibres that I have ever found, drawn out from a piece of cord that I guard with my life! It is so fine and has so many kinks in it that it is extremely difficult to handle. Dealing with it is made easier by twisting a length of fine wire into a loop. The twists are sealed with thin CA glue and the loose ends trimmed off. The end of the fibre can be passed through the loop, which is then used like a needle. The fibre can simply be threaded where I want it to go, over yards, between other fibres, through the railings, and finally pulled gently to take up the slack and held in place with the Blu-Tack.

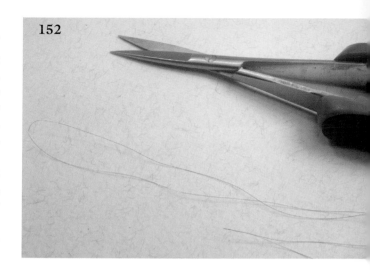

152

153.

When pulling a fine fibre out from the cord, it is important to keep control of the end, which will tend to float off on any air current. I secured the first end in the Blu-Tack in front of the bows straightaway, pulled out the rest of the fibre and threaded the second end through the wire loop. I then had a fair degree of control. Using the wire loop like a bendy sewing needle, the fibre has been passed over the top of the lower yard on the foremast, through the railings at the aft end of the bridge, back over the yard, and down again to the same lump of Blu-Tack. I took care to pull the knots out of the fibre, which form whenever it is slack and enabled to coil up. When everything was sufficiently tight, and the fibres positioned correctly along the yard, I applied gum to the yard. I will shortly cut off the waste. It will be noted that I have fixed the lifts from the mast to the ends of the yard. Doing this first also helps me keep control of the fibre, which would otherwise slip off the end of the yard.

153

154.

154.

For the aerials I have used a slightly thicker fibre. It is led from the Blu-Tack at one end of the ship, over the ends of both yards, and down to Blu-Tack at the other end. Nothing could be simpler.

155.

This is just to prove that it isn't all going to collapse. The loose ends have been cut off and the rigging is still in place. I don't think I could lift the whole model on the rigging, but I wouldn't want to, anyway. Nevertheless, the gum is quite strong enough to do the job I want it to.

155

156.

Here I am showing you a method for fitting funnel guys. I have drilled four fine holes in the deck, using the flexible drill that I showed earlier in the book. I have inserted a piece of Caenis into the hole, followed by a short length of stretched sprue, in order to wedge it somewhat. A drop of thin CA glue secures the whole lot, and the excess sprue is trimmed off with a sharp blade.

156

157

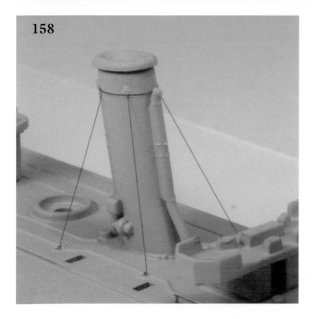

158

157.

I put a small piece of Blu-Tack of top of the funnel, and led the four Caenis threads up to it, so that each is in roughly the correct position. I then took a loop of Caenis and passed it around the top of the funnel. I draw it tight at the height at which the guys attach to the funnel, so that the four threads are drawn into contact with it and held firmly.

158.

After a little adjusting of position and tension, I glued around the loop of Caenis with thin CA. Now that the loose ends have been cut off, some cleaning up of glue spots will be necessary, just above the ends of the funnel guys.

159

159.

160.

This is what it looks like on the finished model of *Sydney*. It is just possible to make out the variation in rigging diameter. The signal halliards are looped around the railing at the aft of the signal deck. Blobs of PVA glue, painted black, are used as insulators. The signal flags are painted onto cigarette paper.

The aerial leads were one of the areas for which I used CA. The fibres were secured into the aerial trunk first. Each lead was taken up in turn and held against its corresponding aerial under very slight tension, and then secured with thin CA before it was trimmed off closely.

160

It does not matter how hard you try, some of the fibres will end up slack, but they can be tightened by judicious application of heat. Some modellers use a lighted cigarette, others a hairdryer. Jim Baumann uses an incense stick. (Ah, memories of university. 'Hey man, don't Bogart that joint!') I use a boring old soldering iron. Simply hold the model upside down, perhaps resting it on a firm object if your hands shake, and bring the heated iron up underneath the droopy fibres, which will then miraculously taughten up. Disaster awaits the reckless with an iron that is brought too close!

⤳ *Cage aerials* ⤳

Cage aerials were a typical feature of warships during the early 20th century, when wireless communication was in its infancy. They consisted of a delicate and complicated arrangement of parallel wires, separated by spacers, shaped either as rings, crosses or six-pointed stars. These are often shown on builder's models, but their representation on models as small as 1/700 has proved almost

impossible until recently. I would regard it as the Holy Grail of small-scale ship modelling. Some modellers have tried taking photo-etched railings and rolling them lengthwise into a long and narrow cylinder. Amazing though this feat may have been, the result looked very solid, but it was a useful experiment along the way, nonetheless.

Mike McCabe replicated cage aerials on his model of HMS *Dreadnought* (see gallery section at www.modelwarships.com), using fishing line, stretched sprue and a jig. He has even used cross-shaped spacers. His effect is extremely convincing, but the idea of moving a completed aerial arrangement from jig to model sounds a bit too trying on the sanity. I believe the method that I have devised is simpler to achieve, and probably more robust. So far I have only been able to do it with ring shaped spacers, but 'watch this space'.

161.

My model of HMS *Cumberland*, with cage aerials.

161

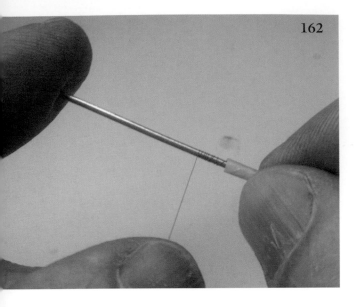

162.

The first thing to do is to make a sufficient number of rings for the spacers. I have used wire from the core of speaker cable. The copper colour needs to be taken off it. This can be done by running the wire over the tip of a black permanent marker pen. It will improve the appearance somewhat, but the coating is not very tough and tends to rub off. I have recently acquired a product called 'Blacken-It', which gives a much more satisfactory finish, but is horribly toxic. To form the rings, I wind the wire tightly around a piece of 1.2mm-diameter brass rod. The end of the wire is fastened to the rod with the masking tape to make it a simple exercise to keep sufficient tension to form the rings.

163.

By running a sharp blade down the length of the rod and cutting each turn of the wire, you will end up with a collection of open rings, all of an equal size and just about perfect circles. Between my fingers can be seen some that I made a few minutes earlier. I would suggest that it is a good idea to close the rings and glue the ends together. Pick up a ring with a pair of fine tweezers. Under a good light, gently 'persuade' the ends together with a fingertip, and then apply a tiny drop of diluted PVA with a fine paintbrush. I always lose a number of rings while doing this, so I cut more than I need in the first place. Producing the rings for my model of HMS *Cumberland* took a couple of hours.

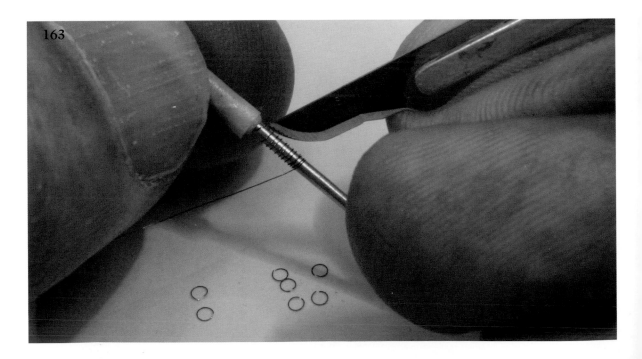

164

164.

The cage aerial is built up directly on the masts of the model, thus requiring a minimal amount of handling. I first mounted two vertical pieces of plastic rod in lumps of Blu-Tack. These must be positioned exactly in the line of the aerial, because they are going to act as spacers to keep a suitable distance between the wires. Choose rod that is the same diameter as the brass rod around which the rings were wound. I then rigged two fibres in exactly

the same way as I showed for the single aerials. One fibre goes on each side of the spacers, but they cross the yards at exactly the same positions. I have glued the fibres to the yard with gum, but I shall not cut the ends until the whole procedure is finished. If this were a proper modelling project, I should use the fine fibres that I used for the signal halliards. For clarity in this demonstration, I am using fibres that are a bit thicker.

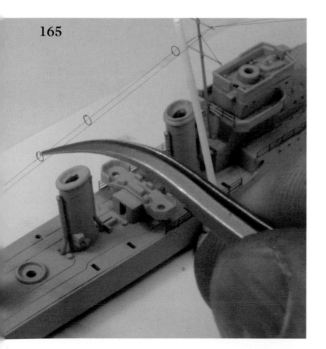

165

165.

What I have got so far is the lower pair of wires for the aerial, and the rings must be glued so that they sit vertically on top of them. I take a fine brush with some gum, undiluted this time, and deposit a tiny droplet on each fibre, at the position where I want a ring to go. I then place the ring into the gum, taking care that it is going straight across between the fibres. It will need to be supported for a minute or so with the tweezers to stop it falling over, but should soon be stable. I fit the rings at each end first of all, and find that this makes it easier to judge equal spacings for the others.

166

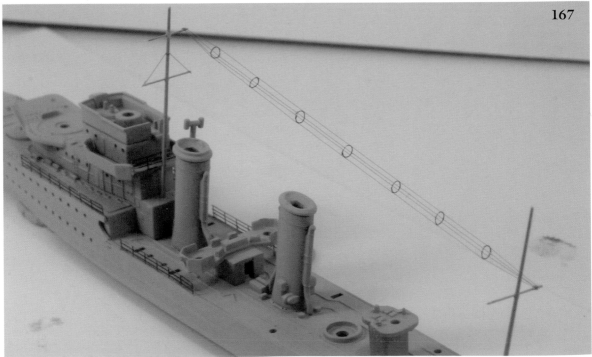

167

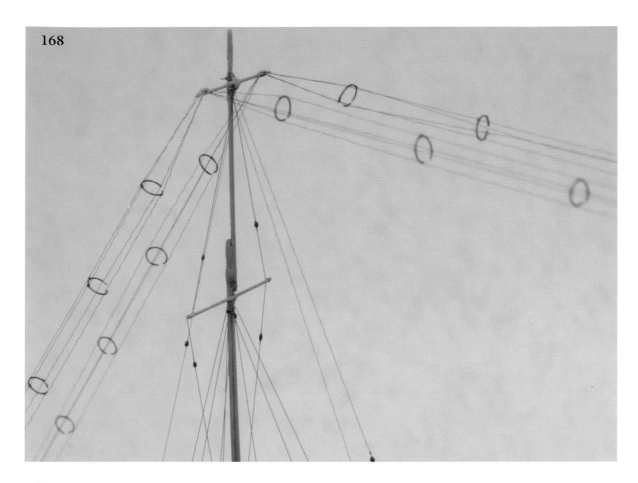

168

166.

The final stage is to fix two upper fibres. Again, one goes on each side of the spacer rods. If I am careful, they should all sit neatly against the upper quarters of each ring. It is more likely that the immutable laws of life will hold true; the fibres are bound to slip down and lodge themselves against the lower fibres that I fixed previously. After careful checking and realignment, I glued the fibres with gum. The joint where the ends of the aerials are fixed to the yards are critical and always going to be subject to some tension. I would not want to trust its integrity to gum alone, and so this is an occasion when I reinforce it by using thin CA glue.

167.

I have removed the spacer rods and cut off the loose ends, and nothing has given way so far. But the aerials will put a fair bit of stress on the yards and masts. I strongly advise that the masts should be replaced with brass rod for this kind of rigging, and that any joints between lower and upper masts should be made by soldering. Do not trust them to CA glue. Believe me, I know! I know more than once!

168.

This is a close-up of the aerials on HMS *Cumberland*. When I displayed this model at the IPMS US National Convention in 2008, it not only won a gold medal and the trophy for 'Best Diorama', but gained a special mention from the head judge for its rigging. I notice on this photo that a couple of the fibres have slipped a bit, and need adjusting and re-gluing. Well, nobody's perfect!

CHAPTER 10

∽Setting the Scene – Bases and Dioramas∽

∽Sea bases for single ships∽

An attractive base sets off the completed model nicely. It demonstrates the modeller's pride in his work, and encourages the viewer to see the model as a work of art rather than just the pointless product of a mere pastime. It also has a practical use, in that it makes a model ship more stable, and easier to handle and store without damage from greasy fingers or contact with other models.

Admittedly, a ship model on a base takes up considerably more shelf space than a model that is not so mounted. For prolific builders with limited room for storage and display, bases might be a luxury that modellers cannot afford for any but their best work. However, if it is possible, I would encourage them to mount models on bases.

I have tried to show techniques for making a ship model appear 'alive'. It seems logical to me that it should be presented to the viewer in its natural environment, namely with the sea coming up to the waterline. I consider it inappropriate to put a model such as this onto a polished wooden base and supported on keel blocks or brass finials,

169.

HMS *Starling* on her base. This base is neither so big that the small ship looks lost, nor a shape that makes the composition feel awkward. I built it to the correct dimensions.

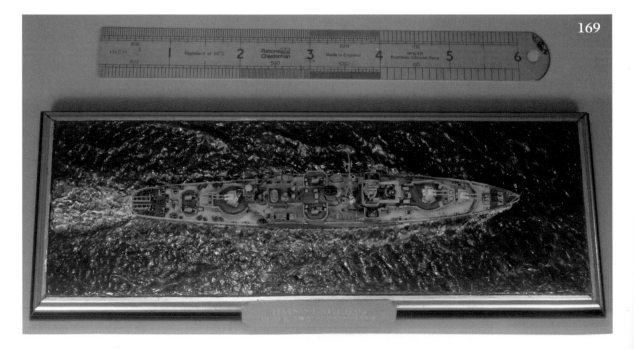

169

which is the correct mode of display for a museum-style model.

It is really quite easy to make a convincing sea base. The materials are readily available from any art shop and are not difficult or hazardous to use.

For a single ship, the base should complement the model, not detract, overpower or distract attention from it. For this reason, it should be the right size and the right shape. As a ship is long and narrow, the base should be too. Models are often mounted on bases that are too square – perhaps commercially made bases that are really intended for aircraft or AFVs. The ship ends up being 'shoe-horned' into the diagonal, with the bow and stern tightly into the corners and a large triangle of water on each beam. One looks at the base, saying 'Ooops!' and ignoring the model. A well-made ship, displayed on its own, requires a base that is built to fit. If there is a base that can be made use of, then plan a suitable diorama for it.

Do not make the base too big. It can be as little as 3cm larger all round than the model for something like a 1/700 cruiser, a bit more for a battleship and smaller for a destroyer or frigate. Do not give more space on either side than is given at the bow and stern, otherwise the proportions will appear wrong. I tend to mount the ship so that it is on the centreline of the base. I usually only mount it off centre if there is something else happening in the model; and then it becomes a diorama, and other considerations apply.

Unless incredibly lucky, a modeller is not going to find a ready-made base that is exactly the right size and shape for the model. It will either have to be self-made or custom built. The latter is not as expensive a proposition as might be imagined. In the UK, a firm such as Armstrong Bases will produce something to specification at a price that represents extremely good value, and no more expensive than their standard shapes.

If making your own, the simplest option would be to find a suitably sized plank of wood, or a piece of MDF. Cut to size, with the edges planed, chamfered, stained and polished – either of these can look attractive without being overpowering. Bear in mind, though, that ordinary wood needs to be fully seasoned, because it has a tendency to warp over time as it dries out.

My own preference is to build a plinth surround

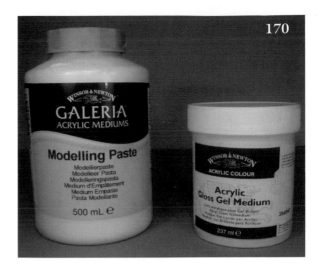

170.

Acrylic paste and gel.

from a picture frame moulding and fix a piece of MDF into it as the mounting surface. This gives a very smart and professional looking finish. But one cannot just go into a picture framer's shop and ask him to make a standard frame 45cm long by 12cm wide. Considering how an ordinary picture frame is constructed, it will be realised that the rebate into which the glass, picture and backing fit, is on the back. If something like this is made for a model base, the baseboard would be fitted in from underneath, and the surface of the water will have a moulded lip all around it. The ship appears as if it is sitting in an enormous 'swimming pool'. It will seem confined and your view of the model from waterline level will be obstructed.

To solve this problem, turn the moulding outwards through 90° before cutting the mitres. The rebate will now appear on the front (or upper) and inner edge of the frame. Unfortunately, the cutting guillotines used by picture framers cannot cope with this change and tend to crush the moulding if it is tried. I therefore buy a length of moulding and do the cutting myself with a sharp saw and a mitre box.

Before moving onto my demonstration of the process, let me tell you about the rest of the materials, and why I choose to use them.

Watercolour paper is glued on top of the

171.

These acrylic paints cost about £1 for a bottle that is five times the size of a tin of modelling paint. Don't try putting most of them through your airbrush, though.

mounting board to the size and shape of the sea surface. This is a very thick paper with a rough texture that can be used as the first stage in representing the ripples on the water.

To build up the waves and ripples I use two types of acrylic paste. Acrylic modelling paste is soft, white and opaque. It goes on easily and can be shaped with a palette knife and damp paintbrush to give the basic shapes of waves and the ship's wake. It takes 24 hours or more to dry fully, depending on thickness, and does tend to shrink a bit.

Acrylic gel medium is a slightly opalescent substance that goes on translucent but sets to a transparent glossy finish that has depth and thickness

to it. This can be used to give a highly convincing effect of ripples. It sets much more quickly.

These are both readily available from any good art shop, and all of the manufacturers of artists' materials make their own brands. There is not much to choose between them. Each tub will cost several pounds but contain enough gel to do anything up to twenty modest-sized bases. If the tub lids are airtight, they will keep for at least three years.

To paint the water, I use the least-expensive acrylic paints that I can get from the art shop. These will not be from the proper artist's range of paints, but from the budget level of craft paints. I tend not to use modelling paints, because the colour of the sea needs to be mixed from fairly pure, bright pigments, rather than those intended for camouflage schemes. These inexpensive paints are also a fraction of the price of standard modelling paints, and I tend to get through quite a lot of the stuff by the time I arrive at the right shade and hue.

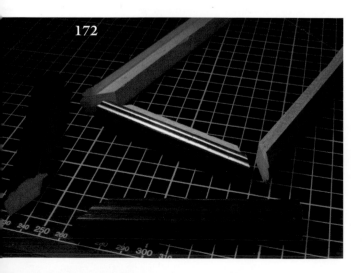

172.

This is the sequence of processes for making the base for the model of *Sydney*. A picture is worth a thousand words, as they say. The two small pieces of moulding have been cut in the normal orientation, as would be appropriate for a picture frame. See how the edge of the frame will be higher than the surface of the sea if they were to be used for a model base. The larger pieces show what I mean by turning the moulding outwards through 90° before cutting. When these are glued up and a sheet of MDF cut to size and inserted, the surface will be level.

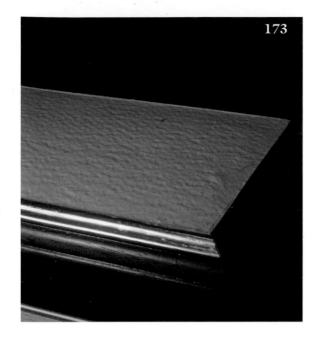

173.

A piece of MDF is glued in place, and watercolour paper is fixed on top using contact adhesive such as Evo-Stik. The low angle of the light shows the texture of the paper. I do not buy the highest quality, hand-made watercolour paper, but I do always get the thickest grade I can find and make sure that it is the texture called 'rough', which speaks for itself. The paper tends to shrink marginally as the glue dries, so I protect the fancy moulding with masking tape, cut the paper over-size and trim it after it has fully dried. The paper also exerts a considerable traction force due to the shrinkage, and this can result in significant warping on a large base. It is not usually a problem with 1/700 models, but for a 1/350 battleship, I would glue another piece of paper to the underside of the mounting board to exert a counter-stress and prevent bending.

174.

I have applied a first layer of acrylic modelling paste to begin building up the basic shape of waves. I painted the watercolour paper grey – this is only to make the white paste show up in the photo; I do not usually do this. At this stage, I am concentrating on the ship's bow wave and wake, with the main sea surface being just random splodges. Looking at photographs of ships will give inspiration as to the real appearance of bow waves as ships move through the water.

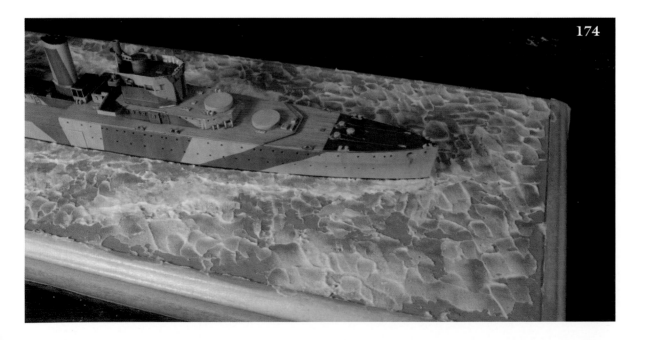

175.

After the first layer has dried for at least 24 hours, I apply a second layer to build up the rest of the sea surface, outside of the area of the bow wave and wake. I try to maintain a visual difference in texture between the two areas, which will be enhanced when painted. I put the paste on with an artist's palette knife, but the shapes achieved with the use of this tool are coarse and crude, and benefit by softening with a moist paintbrush. Avoid getting overenthusiastic and making the waves too big. Bear in mind the scale and remember that a wave ¼in high in this scale will represent something 15ft high in real life. After the paste has fully dried, it might be necessary to add some more around the edge of the ship, as shrinkage might have caused a concave meniscus to form, which is unrealistic.

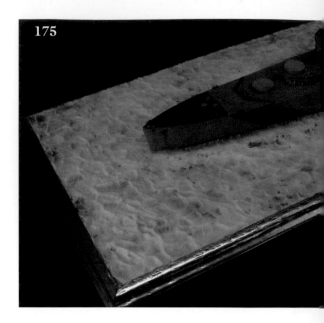

176.

I have completed the basic painting of the sea, having mixed suitable colours from acrylic paints. The model represents the ship in the Mediterranean, where the sun will tend to be hot and the skies clear. The sea will appear dark and blue, as it would in the Pacific. In the North Atlantic, where skies are more likely to be overcast, a paler, greyer and perhaps slightly greener colour would be appropriate. Areas around the ship, in its wake and bow waves, where the water is disturbed or foamy, are painted in a colour that is lighter, brighter and both bluer and greener. Look over the side of a ship or ferry and see what I mean. This colour is also used to highlight the tops of waves over the whole of the base. Finally, paint that is a shade or two darker than the basic mixture is worked into the troughs between the waves, in order to add to the three-dimensional effect.

177.

I apply a layer of acrylic gel medium over the sea surface. Although it comes out of the tub white and translucent, it will dry glossy and transparent. It begins setting very quickly, so do only a few square inches at a time. I spread on a layer about 1–2mm thick with a palette knife. I then take a medium-sized brush, and with a regular flicking motion, pick up a rippled texture in the gel. I try to get all of the ripples oriented in the same direction. I wash the brush frequently with water because the gel will set in it as I work. At the far right of the picture is an area that I have 'rippled', and just above the knife blade is an area yet to be worked over. On the far side of the ship, the gel has already started drying.

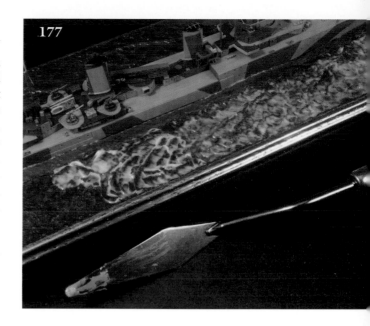

178.

The final stage is adding white paint to represent foam. I have used acrylic paint, and applied several layers. First, diluted paint that allows the blue colour to show through gives the impression of patches of bubbles below the water's surface. Thicker paint looks like foam on top of the water. I used a small brush and put the paint on with a lot of small dots and squiggles that follow the lines of the waves. I have tried not to finish with areas that are evenly and intensely white, because these look unrealistic and lack the appearance of fluidity and movement. Note how the band of water beside the ship has a brighter and bluer appearance than the rest of the sea.

179.

I made the texture of the wake by placing the palette knife flat on the wet gel medium after it had been laid, and lifting it sharply upwards. This gave a random churning of the surface. I painted the foam in the same way as the rest, but there is rather more undiluted paint. This gives the impression of much heavier disturbance from the turning screws. You might wish to paint a coat of gloss varnish over the sea surface. There is debate over whether this is appropriate. It can cause the base to look too glossy, as real sea, with all its ripples, reflects the light randomly and does not have a mirror-like quality. However, with an airbrushing of a final coat of matt varnish over the model, any overspray will cause the sea to be totally matt, which is an equally unrealistic appearance. It might be that a coat of satin varnish is the best choice.

180.

This photo of a White Ensign 1/350 Schnellboote shows an imitation of the wake of a fast-moving boat. The usual method of using fillers results in a solid-looking appearance. Here I have taken torn pieces of toilet paper, only a few millimeters across, and stuck lots of them into puddles of diluted PVA glue until the bow wave and wake were built up large enough. I touched up the tips of the waves with white acrylic paint, because I expected that the paper would eventually turn yellow, which I think is now happening. In the meantime, the effect is pretty good, and the model has power and movement.

∽Dioramas∽

I should now like to share some of my thoughts about the art of diorama building, and illustrate it with photos of some of the (not so remarkable) dioramas that I have made and other much finer examples made by friends. I am not going to try and describe in detail how to go about making dioramas, because it is a subject broad enough for a book in its own right, and I do not consider myself to be a great exponent of the genre.

I do, however, think that I am qualified to say what makes a suitable subject, how it should tell its story, and what makes some dioramas work better than others. It follows that this chapter is purely my own opinion, and I respect other modellers' right to disagree strongly, if they wish.

Precise definitions of what constitutes a diorama are mainly of use to competition judges who must be able to justify why a particular model should be in this or that class. Usually, the definitions centre on the model being presented on more than a 'plain' base, or there being more than just crew figures included, or more than one piece of equipment. In our case, this means more than one ship. The American IPMS rules mention merit being given for strength of story-telling or illustration of a theme, but apart from this, rules do not give any guidance as to what makes a 'good' diorama. This is something that is very subjective.

Sometimes the rules can seem perverse and illogical. I had friendly arguments over several years with the competition organiser at the Scottish IPMS Nationals, who insisted that my ships should be classed as dioramas, simply because they had crew figures on their decks, although the bases were of plain sea and no other vessels, boats or other activities were depicted. I pointed out that if the presence of crew figures determined whether a model was a diorama, then it logically followed that every model of a tank that had its commander's head poking out of the hatch ought also to be classed as a diorama. It may seem a small point, but it meant that my models were placed in a much smaller class and up against weaker competition.

These rules and strict definitions only matter in the context of competitions, and even then we

ought not to take them too seriously. For most of us, modelling is only a hobby and the world will not stop turning because of it.

Returning to my thoughts on dioramas. We are, first, trying to replicate real life. This is what I have been showing how to do, with the use of delicate details, rigging and subtle use of paints. But in planning a diorama, the modeller needs to be doing more than that. However well built and painted it is, a ship on a sea base is not a diorama. It needs to have a context.

I suggest that there are a number of features, which, if incorporated into a model, will turn it into a diorama. There is no need to have all of these, just a single feature might be enough to justify the term, although with two or three a much stronger composition will result. If an attempt is made to have every single feature, there is a risk of producing something that is too 'busy' and loses focus on its central theme.

The features include:

- more than one ship, or extra smaller vessels;
- shoreline or dockside;
- depiction of a relationship between vessels;
- human activity;
- industrial, military or naval activity;
- combat;
- depiction of a dramatic incident, either historical or imaginary;
- reproduction of some famous photograph or painting; and
- depiction of an emotion.

Similar features would apply to the dioramas that are made by our colleagues in the armour-modelling fraternity, and they have some advantages over ship modellers. Vehicles can pass very close to each other and can therefore be shown in company on a base of reasonable size. Land combat can take place at close quarters and is a suitable diorama subject for the same reason. When representing the human body at a scale of 1/35 or even 1/76, one can show posture, gesture and even facial expression. The human element in a diorama can come across easily.

Turn the equation round the other way and matters of scale, size and distance put restrictions on ship modellers. When underway, ships try to keep a sensible distance between one another, and a scene showing two full size vessels proceeding at speed on a small base would result, in real life, in the commanding officers being court martialled! Trying to show two ships in combat at realistic ranges would need a base many yards across.

Showing human activity in 1/700 scale is difficult to do convincingly because most of the photo-etched frets of crew figures have stiff and stereotyped poses. I find it impossible to imagine that at any one moment 10% of the crew would be saluting!

Putting these difficulties to one side, consider the types of ideas that might give inspiration for dioramas, and what opportunities or pitfalls these might bring.

One ought to avoid putting two ships moving together unless there is a good reason for them to be very close. Depicting the process of underway replenishment is a good example and would also show human and naval activity as well as emphasising a relationship between the vessels. Scratch-builders might be tempted by the accidental ramming of HMS *Victoria* by HMS *Camperdown* in 1893.

Having small craft around a larger vessel is another matter entirely. Ship's boats, tugs, harbour craft such as lighters, oilers, colliers and victualling craft; any of these can be dancing in attendance on their larger mistress. Even pleasure craft could be shown having a nose around with people waving to the crew.

It would be quite appropriate to have two or more ships in a dockside setting. So many things may be happening that there is scope for endless fun. But beware: it is all too possible to get carried away. It is my firm belief that a good diorama ought to have a strong central theme or story, and a bustling dockside scene might fail to have one, or lose it among all the small details.

Showing a combat situation is likely to be more convincing if only one ship is used. For example, take a US destroyer, at full speed, and heeling heavily as it executes a tight evasive turn. All of its guns and directors, as well as the attention of every crew member are aimed at one point in the sky, from which the viewer is invited to imagine the kamikaze attack is coming.

National pride or sensitivity will play an important part in choice of combat subject. As a Brit, I have every intention of portraying HMS *Campbeltown*, her decks crowded with khaki marines and in the process of changing from a German ensign to the White Ensign. Or what about the 'little ships' at Dunkirk, or the death throes of *Ark Royal*?

I expect that American modellers would tend to choose subjects from their own naval heritage, Pearl Harbor coming immediately to mind, or perhaps USS *Ward* if there is the wish to keep things simple. Another dramatic idea might be USS *Birmingham* alongside the crippled *Princeton*. For the Japanese surrender ceremony on board USS *Missouri*, it is possible to buy a complete fret of photo-etched figures, camera and tripod included, I believe.

An RNLI lifeboat could show drama and emotion rescuing crew from a foundering merchantman in a heavy storm. This might be a fitting tribute to the courageous and unpaid volunteers who man these boats and sometimes make the ultimate sacrifice for others.

I believe it is possible to show emotion without any human presence at all, if it is possible to imbue the vessels with their own strong personalities. Imagine a rotting, derelict wooden pier, perhaps with a tumbledown shack on the end. Tied up alongside are two forgotten tugboats, windows broken, doors and hatches open, paint faded and rust of various colours on every metal surface. Nobody has trodden their decks for years and even the shipbreaker doesn't want to know. The only 'friends' these vessels have are each other, and maybe the gulls depositing their guano. The atmosphere of neglect and desolation is heightened by the very absence of any human figure from the scene. I'm so taken by this idea that I'm already planning on how I can scratch-build some tugboats!

Inspiration for similar dioramas might be found in photos of once-proud warships being broken up in the years following the the Second World War.

A good diorama can draw attention into it, and then cause the eye to travel around the composition, moving from one area to another.

181.

The way to do this is to have a small number of points of interest, or one major point and some subsidiary. If the diorama has a particularly important focus of activity or interest, I advise that positioning it near to the centre of the composition is avoided. That might seem a bit perverse, but if the eye is immediately drawn to the centre, it will tend to remain static, and become bored quickly. Have a major focus, and the other minor foci off-centre, but do not go the other way and put these too close to the edges.

When photographers and artists arrange their compositions they often adhere to the 'rule of thirds'. If a picture has two equidistant vertical lines drawn on it, at one third and two thirds of its length, and two similar horizontal lines, there will be four points of intersection, each one third of the way from both end and side. These are the best places to position the major features of the picture, and there are numerous examples of this in the history of art.

This same rule can be applied when planning dioramas. I don't suggest that it must always be slavishly followed. I don't consciously follow it when I am planning a diorama, but I find that if it is successful, the major features are often found around one or more of these points.

181.

Let's start taking a look at some photos of dioramas, some of mine and some made by friends, and consider what makes them good or not so good. This model of HMS *Hood*, by Tamiya, was made several years ago and was among the first ships I did. It is now very much the worse for wear. I include it here as an example of a thoroughly bad diorama. Although it won a gold medal at the Nationals, I now think it did not deserve it. The presence of the Admiral's barge and the picket boat make it 'technically' a diorama, but if they were taken out it would not really detract from the model. There is still too much water surface, and the main activity, piping aboard the Admiral prior to her final sortie against *Bismarck*, hardly grabs the attention. I reckon that any merit it had was in the way I learned to do the rigging and coping with Gold Medal railings. But then every model is a step on an educational journey.

182

183

182.

In contrast, this does work well. It represents one of the Elco PT boats that defended the Philippines in early 1942. It is actually the only dockside diorama that I have ever made. A diorama does not have to be big. This is just 4in square. The moulding of the PT boat by MS Models of St Petersburg is just exquisite, as is that of the whaleboat by L'Arsenal, which also produced the figures. Although it does not quite follow the rule of thirds, the eye tends to be drawn in a circle, from the officers talking, to the men in the whaleboat, to the guys sitting fishing on the bows, and I believe that this is why it is successful.

183.

Mike McCabe sent me this photo of his diorama of the Argentinean aviso *Commandante General Zapiola*. As with my Elco, it is only about 4in square, and I regard it as one of the most perfect little dioramas I have seen. She is delivering supplies to an isolated and frozen scientific station somewhere in Tierra del Fuego. That really is at the ends of the Earth! It tells its story beautifully, and I think it manages to say much more than its small size should really allow. (Photo by Mike McCabe)

184.

I believe that a model of a single ship, without any other scenery, craft or artefacts, might still be a diorama, if it has a story. Here is Combrig's model of the battleship *Potemkin* in 1905. Towards the end of the mutiny, she encountered the rest of the Black Sea Fleet, and sailed along the line of the other ships, which had their guns trained upon her. Fully expecting to be fired upon, *Potemkin*'s crew cheered to their comrades in the rest of the fleet, who were also close to mutiny. Note the colour of the funnels. Although the official scheme called for them to be painted an ochre colour, a photograph of *Potemkin* during the mutiny shows unequivocally that hers were white.

185

"We a' gang doon the watter,
tae see that splendid cat"
HMS TIGER ON THE CLYDE. 1914

186

185.

Combrig's kit of the battlecruiser HMS *Tiger* is a beautiful model of a beautiful ship. Oscar Parkes describes how sailors would row miles just to catch a look at her, and I postulate that the paddle steamers on the Clyde might have done the same. The little generic steamer was scratch built from plans that I found in an old copy of *Model Shipwright*. The theme is carried through in the title of the composition, 'We a' gang doon the watter, tae see that splendid cat'. People in Scotland seem to think that the paddle steamer is *Waverley*, which it most definitely is not. The paddle steamer seems to be at the position of thirds, and the crew figures on *Tiger*'s fo'c'sle are at a roughly corresponding position.

186.

This is another of Mike McCabe's models. This uses the White Ensign 1/700 kit to represent 'Johnnie' Walker's HMS *Starling* returning to the docks in Liverpool after another successful hunting expedition. I believe it is based on a famous photograph of this occasion. The quay is crowded with cheering and waving people. This is one of those times where it is an advantage to have photo-etched figures with raised arms! It is not obvious in this photograph, but Mike's water technique is just about the most realistic that I have seen anywhere. (Photo by Mike McCabe.)

187

187.

I include this photo as another example of a single ship as a diorama. On this White Ensign 1/350 Flaklighter, the main guns, rangefinder and the attention of the officers on the bridge are all directed to a single point, way outside of the base area. This is a similar idea to that of the US destroyer evading the kamikaze attack referred to above.

188

189

188.

Jim Baumann is a true master of 1/700 ship modelling. His harbour diorama built around a Hog Islander-type merchant ship by Battlefleet Models is a *tour de force* in respect of construction, detailing and painting. But he tells me that he kept being supplied with more bits and pieces, so the composition kept growing and growing. Unfortunately, this has resulting in the diorama, as a whole, losing focus, because there is so much to look at. (Photo by Jim Baumann)

189.

Peter Fulgoney has made his own diorama using the same Hog Islander kit. It has simpler composition than Jim's, and in my opinion works better. There is an obvious main focus for the attention, with the tugs nudging the ship away from the quayside. But there is still plenty more to look at. (Photo by Peter Fulgoney)

190.

This is another diorama by Jim Baumann, and I think that it works incredibly well. Combrig's French battleship *Henri IV* is surrounded by sailing craft of all kinds, and the composition is a swirl of movement and life. Being a sailor, Jim has ensured that the sails are set correctly for the directions in which they are heading. (Photo by Jim Baumann)

L'Arsenal
Boite Postale No 2
14790 Verson
France

Manufacturers of resin kits and accessories as well as photo-etch.

Micro-Mark Tools
Website: www.micromark.com

A major American Internet supplier of tools for modellers.

Armstrong Bases
Olive House
Seaside Lane
Easington
County Durham
SR8 3PG
UK

Tel: +44 (0)191 527 0532
Mobile: +44 (0)7940 524569
Email: armstrong-bases@hotmail.co.uk

The ideal place to go for a custom-made base in the UK. Very good value for money.

Glasgow Angling Centre
Unit 1, The Point Retail Park
29 Saracen St
Glasgow
G22 5HT
UK

Tel: +44 (0)141 331 6330
Website: www.fishingmegastore.com

This is where I first discovered 'Caenis' thread.

J Stockard, Fly Fishing
14 Flanders Lane
PO Box 800
Kent
CT 06757-0800
USA

Tel: +1 (877) 359 8946
    +1 (860) 927 1100
Website: www.jsflyfishing.com

If you cannot get it 'Caenis' in the UK, you will certainly get from the United States.

Wires.Co.UK
18 Raven Rd
South Woodford
London
E18 1HW
UK

Tel: +44 (0)20 8505 0002
Website: www.wires.co.uk

An online supplier of small quantities of wire in a variety of metals and alloys, in sizes down to the finest imaginable.

International Plastic Modellers' Society
Website (UK): www.ipms-uk.co.uk

In a word, join.